INSIGHT GUIDES

CROATIA
StepbyStep

APA PUBLICATIONS | L
Part of the Langenscheidt Publishing Group

CONTENTS

ABOUT THIS BOOK

This *Step by Step Guide* has been produced by the editors of Insight Guides, whose books have set the standard for visual travel guides since 1970. With top-quality photography and authoritative recommendations, this guidebook brings you the very best of Croatia in a series of 15 tailor-made tours.

WALKS AND TOURS

The tours in the book provide something to suit all budgets, tastes and trip lengths. Whether you like to visit remote islands or prefer the cultural attractions and buzz of a major city, are keenly interested in archaeology and architecture or prefer to chill out at the beach, you will find an option to suit. The tours cover Croatia's classic attractions, as well as ones located off the beaten track, and include travelling by boat, car, bicycle and on foot.

We recommend that you read the whole of a tour before setting out. This should help you to familiarise yourself with the route and enable you to plan where to stop for refreshments – options for this are shown in the

Above: Dolac market, Zagreb; vestibule of Diocletian's Palace, Split; Makarska; handrail in the Rector's Palace, Dubrovnik; fishing boat, Hvar.

'Food and Drink' boxes, recognisable by the knife-and-fork sign, on most pages.

For our pick of the walks by theme, consult Recommended Tours For… *(see pp.6–7)*.

OVERVIEW

The tours are set in context by this introductory section, giving an overview of the country to set the scene, plus background information on food and drink, shopping, entertainment and outdoor activities. A succinct timeline in this chapter highlights the key events that have shaped Croatia's history.

DIRECTORY

Also supporting the tours is a Directory chapter, comprising a user-friendly, clearly organised A–Z of practical information, our pick of where to stay while you are in the country and select restaurant listings (complementing the more low-key cafés and restaurants that feature within the tours themselves), and recommended nightlife and entertainment venues.

The Authors

Jeanne Oliver is a freelance writer based in France. She first visited Croatia in 1996, not too long after Croatia had become the world's newest country. Captivated by the mixture of Slavic and Mediterranean culture, endless coastline, hearty cuisine and unpretentious lifestyle, she has returned nearly every year since. Even as her travel-writing career took her to myriad other destinations in Europe, Croatia's ever-evolving scene has continued to fascinate her. Jeanne helps others plan their trip to Croatia with her online guide www.croatiatraveller.com.

Many of the tours in this book were originally conceived by Croatia specialist Jane Foster.

Margin Tips

Shopping tips, historical facts, handy hints and information on activities help visitors make the most of their time in Croatia.

Feature Boxes

Notable topics are highlighted in these special boxes.

Key Facts Box

This box gives details of the distance covered on the tour, plus an estimate of how long it should take. It also states where the tour starts and finishes, and gives key travel information such as which days are best to do the tour or handy transport tips.

Route Map

Detailed cartography shows the tour clearly plotted with numbered dots. For more detailed mapping, see the pull-out map slotted inside the back cover.

Food and Drink

Recommendations of where to stop for refreshment are given in these boxes. The numbers prior to each restaurant/café name link to references in the main text. The restaurants are also plotted on the tour maps.

The € signs at the end of each entry reflect the approximate cost of a meal for two with a glass of house wine. These should be seen as a guide only. Price ranges, also quoted on the inside back flap for easy reference, are as follows:

€€€€	over 400Kn
€€€	250–400Kn
€€	150–250Kn
€	below 150Kn

Footers

Look here for the tour name, a map reference and the main attraction on the double page.

ARCHITECTURE

Encircled by its ramparts, Dubrovnik (tour 12) is architecturally unique. Rovinj (tour 5), Trogir (tour 8), Hvar (tour 11) and Korčula (tour 15) are Renaissance jewels, while Zagreb (tours 1 and 2) is a mix of the Middle Ages and the 19th century.

RECOMMENDED TOURS FOR...

OUTDOOR TYPES

Work up a sweat climbing Biokovo Mountain (tour 8), or for a gentler workout, swim and cycle on Mljet (tour 13) or Hvar (tour 11). Rovinj (tour 5) offers several activities: rock-climbing, scuba-diving and swimming.

SHOPPERS

Zagreb (tours 1 and 2) is the place to catch up with the latest fashions and buy wine and food products from around the country. Split (tour 7) and Dubrovnik (tour 12) are good for handicrafts and markets.

BEACHES

The best sandy beaches are those of Pelješac (tour 14), Lopud (tour 12), Lumbarda on Korčula (tour 15) and the Pakleni Islands (tour 11). Mljet (tour 13) and Vis (tour 10) have quieter options.

NATIONAL PARKS

For unspoilt natural beauty try Krka (tour 9) with its island monastery and waterfalls, the striking Plitvice Lakes (tour 4) and verdant Mljet (tour 13) with two saltwater lakes and lush forests.

FOODIES

A stay in Croatia would not be complete without sampling wine from the Pelješac peninsula (tour 14), truffles from Istria (tour 6), and seafood from the Lim Channel (tour 5) or Mali Ston (tour 14). For fine dining, Zagreb (tours 1 and 2) and Pula (tour 5) have some top restaurants.

ART-LOVERS

The museums of Zagreb (tours 1 and 2) contain a sizeable part of Croatia's heritage. The Meštrović Gallery in Split (tour 7) has an excellent selection of work by Croatia's most renowned sculptor, while Dubrovnik's Dominican Monastery (tour 12) displays art by members of the important Dubrovnik school.

ROMAN RUINS

Diocletian's Palace in Split (tour 7) retains most of the grandeur of the original imperial palace, and Salona (tour 8) is another site whose scale is awe-inspiring. It is easy to imagine gladiatorial combat in the Roman amphitheatre of Pula (tour 5).

CHILDREN

Kids love the beach, but they will also be awed by the waterfalls of Plitvice Lakes (tour 4) and Krka National Park (tour 9). The castles of Zagorje (tour 3) are straight out of a fairy tale.

NIGHT-OWLS

The most diverse nightlife is in Zagreb (tours 1 and 2), with everything from jazz clubs to throbbing discos. Hvar Town (tour 11) has the trendiest cocktail scene, and Split (tour 7) has a Mediterranean vibe with several outdoor venues.

OVERVIEW

An overview of Croatia's geography, customs and culture, plus illuminating background information on food and drink, shopping, entertainment, outdoor activities and history.

INTRODUCTION

Croatia is now one of Europe's most exciting destinations, with a seemingly endless coastline, hundreds of islands and the kind of easygoing attitude that makes for a great holiday. History, culture, beaches: Croatia has it all, and it is easy to get around speaking English.

Above: dalmatian in Dalmatia.

Environment

Respect for the environment is ingrained in the Croatian lifestyle. As heavy industry was never implanted in the country, Croatians have become accustomed to clean water, clean air and clean, locally grown produce. The biggest environmental problem is fire: forest fires regularly ravage the coast and islands during the dry summer season. Also of national concern is the decreasing amount of fish left in the Adriatic, due to overfishing.

Perhaps one of Croatia's best attributes is that you get two countries for the price of one. The long coastal region is heavily influenced by Italy, from the cuisine and Roman ruins to the insouciant attitude. Zagreb and northern Croatia, on the other hand, have much closer cultural, lingual and economic ties with Germany and Austria which are demonstrated, in particular, by the Baroque cities that flourished in the 17th and 18th centuries under Austro-Hungarian rule. This duality is a direct result of Croatia's tortuous history.

Croatian Identity

The great epoch of Croatian kings was over 1,000 years ago. For many centuries a country called 'Croatia' simply didn't exist. The Adriatic coast was part of the Roman Empire and then the Byzantine Empire before bouncing over to Hungarian kings and then the Venetians, the French (under Napoleon Bonaparte), and Italy in the 20th century. Austrians and Hungarians exerted nearly continuous control over the interior until the end of World War I when the first Kingdom of Serbs, Croats and Slovenes emerged, later supplanted by Yugoslavia at the end of World War II *(see also pp.22–3)*. During all of this, a sense of national identity was somehow kept alive throughout Croatia's diverse regions. The Serbian nationalism of Slobodan Milošević provided the spark that fired up Croatia's long-suppressed dream of independence. Nevertheless, the resulting conflagration took most Croatians by surprise. The terrible war years were followed by economic stagnation. But in spite of a long and difficult journey, independent Croatia has regained its footing and anticipates joining the European Union in the not-too-distant future *(see feature, p.13)*.

COUNTRY LAYOUT

Covering 56,538 sq km (21,830 sq miles), Croatia can be divided into three regions: the lowland basin between the Sava and Drava rivers, which includes Zagreb and then rises to the northern hills of the Zagorje; the Dinaric mountains that rise so dramatically from the coast; and the long littoral that stretches along the Adriatic. In terms of popularity among visitors, the coast is a clear winner. From Istria to Dubrovnik, it runs 1,778km (1,105 miles), while 1,185 offshore islands and islets provide innumerable opportunities for sport and relaxation.

Zagreb and Northern Croatia

Too few people spend time in this part of the country. Zagreb has everything you could hope for in a Central European capital: museums, fine restaurants, exciting nightlife and a typical mixture of Baroque and Secessionist architecture. During the Yugoslav years, when Zagreb was playing second fiddle to Belgrade, this repository of Croatian culture languished. Now it is rushing to flash its newfound prosperity. Women in the latest fashions crowd into trendy boutiques or linger over cocktails in sleek cafés, while men in designer sunglasses emerge from Italian sportscars. Yet there is also a more bohemian side, evident in the funky cafés and clubs of Zagreb's medieval Upper Town.

The city makes a great base from which to venture into the cool hills of the Zagorje region to the north. Here the farmers are only a generation removed from cart-and-horse transport. It was from this region that the Croatian nobility once reigned; a visit to their turreted castles is a trip to the heart of the Croatian national identity.

Istria

There are still old-timers in Istria who have lived in four countries without ever leaving their homeland. They were Austrians until 1918, Italians until 1945, Yugoslavs until 1991 and finally Croatians. The turmoil has left Istrians with a philosophical view of history, an agility with languages and a welcoming attitude towards visitors. The last has helped make the region a choice Euro-pean destination for second residences and retirement homes. Of course, a mild climate, reasonable cost of living, delicious food and a long coastline also help Istria's popularity.

Split and the Dalmatian Coast

The inhabitants of Croatia's second city are full of pride. They are proud of their football team, Hadjuk; proud of producing fine tennis players like Goran Ivanišević and Mario Ančić; and proud of the city's easy blend of ancient and modern. The Unesco-protected Diocletian's Palace draws visitors, but the ebullient Split lifestyle keeps them happy. Stroll along the seafront promenade, while away time in a local café, or join the frenetic nightlife scene to understand why Split residents are so passionate about their city.

Split's location makes it easy to sample other choice destinations on the Dalmatian coast, whether your interests

Above from far left: coat of arms of Croatia, Dalmatia and Slavonia on the roof of St Mark's Church in Zagreb; Pakleni Islands off the coast of Hvar; drinks in Zagreb's BP Club.

Below: Split Old Town.

are cultural or lie outdoors. The ancient Roman ruins of Salona are a haunting evocation of a vanished world, and the majestic waterfalls of Krka National Park are an enchanting place to spend the day. The World Heritage Site of Trogir is a jewel of a medieval town, while Makarska lies at the foot of the towering Biokovo Mountain.

Islands

Croatia is the proud possessor of some of the world's most beautiful islands. Years of 'neglect' have made Vis the best get-away-from-it-all island, while Mljet is truly an island paradise with sandy beaches, forested hills and inland lakes. Korčula is steeped in the tradition of cultivating olive trees and vineyards and has a picturesque Old Town to explore. Hvar has lavender fields, an offshore constellation of islands and hyper-trendy nightlife in Hvar Town.

Dubrovnik

The 'pearl of the Adriatic' according to Lord Byron, Dubrovnik is Croatia's crown jewel. The walled city appears to be sculpted rather than built, with monuments, fountains and landmarks of astonishing beauty. A wealth of museums and monasteries trace its fascinating history and unique culture, and it is easy to visit the region it once ruled, such as the Pelješac peninsula with the 'great wall' of Ston or the peaceful Elaphiti Islands.

CLIMATE

As well as two cultures, Croatia also has two distinct climates. Along the coast the climate is Mediterranean, with hot and dry summers, although the mistral blowing from the west refreshes summer afternoons. Winters are rainy, but the Dinaric mountain range protects the coast from harsh weather. The coast from Dubrovnik to Split tends to be one or two degrees warmer than the northern Dalmatian coast up to Istria. Hvar island is the sunniest spot in Croatia.

Inland Croatia has a continental climate. Zagreb and the interior forests are occasionally blanketed with snow, and freezing temperatures are not uncommon from December to the end of February.

WHEN TO GO

Croatia can be appreciated in any season, but most people come in July and August. The weather is reliably sunny, attractions are open longer hours

and there are more boats to whisk you from island to island. May, June and September are less crowded, though, and you can still see and do a lot. By October, many islanders turn from receiving guests to harvesting their olives or grapes, so it is a great time to experience an age-old way of life.

Winter is too cold for swimming in the sea, but Dubrovnik is just as enchanting, and you can share it with residents rather than other tourists. Meanwhile, Zagreb's cultural season is in full swing, and you can ski just outside town. Spring is the best time to visit Plitvice Lakes and Krka National Park, as the cascades are swollen with the melting winter snows.

PEOPLE

Croatia's population has declined from 5 million, when it was part of the former Yugoslavia, to 4.5 million today. During the 1990s war, much of the Serbian population left or was chased out. The return of Serbian refugees has been slow, partly because of the web of legal problems involved in reclaiming their former property. Also, in some parts of the country, bitter feelings and troubled local economies remain from the war years, which means the environment is less than welcoming for returning Serbs.

Religion

Croatians are overwhelmingly – nearly 88 per cent – Roman Catholic. In fact, the defining characteristic of Croats is adherence to the Roman Catholic faith, while Serbs belong to the Eastern Orthodox Church. During the Tito years, religious practices were discouraged if not banned in an attempt to dampen down the nationalistic feelings they so often inspired. Since independence, Croatians have celebrated religious holidays with fervour, and the Catholic Church holds a central place in community life.

Traditions and Customs

Croatians are keen to display their rich cultural heritage. Communities have no trouble in persuading citizens to join in historical re-enactments, participate in folk-dancing events and keep alive the traditions of the forefathers, which differ between regions and sometimes even between islands. Many local festivities take place around Easter, and are connected with local saints' days and historical events. One of the most colourful local displays is the weekly Moreška Sword Dance in Korčula.

Youthful Exodus
Another challenge to population stability is the increasing desire of young people to look for opportunities abroad. Croatia has a long history of exporting its people, from political refugees fleeing Tito to providing labour for the growing post-war economies of Italy and Germany. Croatia's historical ties abroad make it easy for multilingual young people to find higher-paid jobs elsewhere, and many of them choose to do so.

EU Accession

Negotiations for Croatia's accession to the EU began in 2005, even as many Croatians began to have concerns about Croatia's autonomy within Europe. Acceding to EU demands, Croatia has found and prosecuted war criminals from the 1990s war and has made some arrangements for the return of Serb refugees. The government compromised in a bitter dispute with Italy and Slovenia over fishing rights in the northern Adriatic. The public has accepted many concessions, however grudgingly, out of a sense that Croatia's economic prosperity is best assured as an EU member. Unemployment remains high, and many parts of the country have not fully recovered since the war. As matters stand, Croatia expects to become part of the EU in 2011.

FOOD AND DRINK

From fresh fish and locally produced olive oil to fine wines and garden-fresh vegetables, Croatian cuisine is simple but delicious and healthy. Moreover, you can eat and drink extraordinarily well on a reasonable budget.

Bell Stew
In Dalmatia and Istria you are likely to hear of *peka* or *čirepnja*. This is a traditional method of stewing meat and vegetables beneath a bell-like dome buried in hot embers. Most restaurants offering *peka* require your order a day in advance – usually for a minimum of four diners.

Many people are surprised by the quality of Croatian cuisine, which differs between what you can eat on the coast and what you will find on menus around Zagreb. Along the Adriatic, the Italian influence is evident in the excellent pizza and pasta dishes that are everywhere; the menus also emphasise the bounty of the sea with a profusion of fish and seafood dishes. In the interior the menus are much more Central European, with hearty stewed and roasted meat dishes and cream pastries.

WHERE TO EAT

In addition to restaurants, there are also family-run establishments called *gostionice* or *konobe*. A typical *konoba* (or *klet* in Zagorje) can be anything from a small enterprise serving local wine and salty delicacies such as *slane srdele* (salted sardines), *dalmatinski pršut* (Dalmatian ham) and *sir* (cheese) to a full-blown restaurant, though usually with a simple menu often based on the freshest local produce.

Be aware that a *pivnica* is an informal pub that usually does not serve food, and a *kavana* is a café that only serves drinks, cakes and ice cream. You can also satisfy your sweet tooth in a *slasticarna*, which offers cake, strudel and ice cream to take away.

Below: *štrukli* from Zagorje; prawns fresh from the Adriatic.

WHAT TO EAT

For breakfast, try a *burek*, a meat- or cheese-filled pastry; except in touristy areas, it is impossible to find anything resembling an English breakfast.

Seafood

In Istria and Dalmatia, seafood tops the menu, and fish and shellfish are invariably prepared with abundant quantities of olive oil, parsley and garlic and washed down with white wine. Favourite starters include *salat od hobotnice* (octopus salad) and *dagnje* (mussels). In the Limska kanal region of Istria and Mali Ston in Dalmatia, you will also find *oštrige* (oysters). *Crni rižot*, a delicious black risotto cooked in cuttlefish ink, or the more delicate *škampi rižot* made with shrimps' tails, can be found on almost every menu.

Fish come in two categories: class I covers white fish such as *ubatac orada* (gilthead), *šampier* (John Dory), *trilja* (red mullet), *škarpina* (grouper) and *arbun* (sea bream), while class II encompasses the cheaper 'blue' fish, notably *tunj* (tuna), *skuše* (mackerel) and *srdele* (sardines). Fish of both types are often prepared on a *roštilj* (barbecue), and served with a *mješenji salat* (mixed salad) or with *blitva* (swiss chard smothered in olive oil and garlic). *Ligne* (squid),

škampi na buzara (shrimps cooked in tomato sauce) and *brodet* (robust fish soup) are also regular favourites. Mljet is known for its excellent *jastog* (lobster).

Meat

Croatian meat is locally produced – often coming from free-range animals – and *janjetina* (lamb) is the most popular type: in the hinterland roadside restaurants often display whole lambs roasting on a spit. Zagorje is renowned for *purica* (turkey), *patka* (duck) and *guska* (goose), often served with *mlinci* (baked noodles). Other notable meat dishes are the spicy Hungarian *gulaš*, and *pašticada*, a Dalmatian beef stew.

Vegetarians

Vegetarianism has not made much headway here, and while vegetarians can eat well, they do not have a lot to choose from. Nevertheless, simply prepared, locally grown vegetables topped with local olive oil are very flavourful. Salads are on most menus, and vegetable pizzas are readily available.

Dessert

The most popular Croatian desserts include *palačinke* (pancakes), topped with chocolate, walnuts, ice cream or other treats, and various *štrudle* (pies) filled with *jabuka* (apple), *trešnja* (cherry) or *sir* (cheese). *Štrukli*, made from curd cheese folded into a dough, then boiled and served with toasted or fried breadcrumbs, is a speciality of Zagorje. Try salty *štrukli* as a starter and sugary *štrukli* for dessert. *Sladoled* (ice cream) is almost as popular on the eastern Adriatic as in

Italy. The Turks brought baklava to the Balkans, as well as *burek* (cheese baked in filo pastry) and *ćevapčići* (mixed meat kebabs). These two are especially good as cheap takeaway snacks.

WHAT TO DRINK

Croatians are apt to start the day with a strong cup of espresso or cappuccino. In hot weather, it is common to linger over an iced Nescafé – cold coffee with milk and ice cream.

Meals often start with a small glass of *rakija*, made from distilled alcohol flavoured with fruits or herbs. The best-known are Travarica, which takes its taste from aromatic grasses, and Pelinkovac, which is amber-coloured and bitter. The speciality on Vis is carob-based *rogačica*, while in inland Istria you will come across *biska*, made from mistletoe. In Lika (the mountainous central region that includes the Plitvice Lakes), try plum-based *šljivovica*.

The best Istrian wines are the white Malvazija and the red Teran. Dalmatian wines tend to be heavier and have a higher alcohol content. The best-known are the full-bodied reds: Dingač from Pelješac peninsula, and Plavac from Hvar and Vis. The best whites are Pošip Čara from Hvar and Grk from Korčula. To finish the meal, it is customary to take a glass of Prošek, a sweet wine made from sun-dried grapes.

Beer-drinkers can try the two major brands: Ožujsko from Zagreb and Karlovačko from Karlovac, south of the capital. Tap water is drinkable, but bottled water is cheap and readily available.

Above from far left: Zagreb is awash with outdoor cafés; octopus salad; a typical *konoba* will serve fresh local fare; an Istrian spread.

Merenda

This cut-price brunch features *kobasice* (sausage) and *kiseli kupus* (sauerkraut), *tripice* (tripe) or *bakalar* (salted cod). The meal was originally intended for fishermen returning from a hard night on the sea; not everyone's stomach is up to a feast like this so early in the day, which is why the custom is dying out.

Mealtimes

Mealtimes are almost any time of the day. Unlike many other countries, you are not confined to strict lunch hours and dinner hours; you can eat a full meal any time from noon to midnight. Many Croatians work from 7am to 3pm and will eat lunch then. Others take a standard lunch hour. Only in the priciest restaurants is there no meal service between 3 and 7pm.

SHOPPING

There are designer and international brands available, but uniquely Croatian items offer better value for money. Souvenirs are of most interest to most visitors, from textiles to jewellery, and ceramics to perfumes.

The Croatian manufacturing industry all but collapsed after the 1990s war: cosmetics, clothes and household goods are now largely imported, hence the extremely high prices and a tottering national economy. Many Croatians take 'shopping buses' to Trieste in Italy and Graz in Austria; before Christmas there is even a 'shopping ferry' to Ancona in Italy. Nevertheless, you will find excellent food and drink, as well as various traditional handmade products that make unusual gifts to take home.

Below: Giancarlo Zigante, purveyor of truffles. Zigante holds the record for finding the largest truffle in the world.

WINE AND SPIRITS

Croatia has been cultivating grapes since the Roman era, and the quality of wine can be excellent *(see p.15)*.

You will find a wide range of Croatian wines and *rakija* in Vinoteka Bornstein (Kaptol 19) in Zagreb, all beautifully displayed in a large vaulted brick cellar. In Istria, try Epvlon (Eufrazijeva 31) in the Old Town in Poreč, which stays open until 11pm in summer. In Split, call in at Enoteca Terra (Braće Kaliterne 6) close to Bačvica Bay, which is both a shop and a wine bar where you can taste before you buy. In Dubrovnik, Dubro-vačka Kuća (Sv. Dominika 2; www.dubrovacka-kuca.com) sells wine, *rakija* and olive oil.

FOOD

Other foodstuffs include *pršut* (ham) and *Paški sir* (sheep's cheese from the island of Pag). Check customs restrictions before you bring them home, though. Along the coast you can buy *maslinovo ulje* (olive oil), although it is more expensive here than in Italy. For the best deal, go direct to a producer, who will let you try some before you decide whether or not to buy. Truffles are good value, however, and connoisseurs can choose from both the black

and the white varieties of this earthy delicacy that are an Istrian speciality. Indeed, the world's biggest truffle, weighing 1.31kg (3lb) was found by Giancarlo Zigante near Buje in Istria in 1999. Look out for Zigante Tartufi shops in a number of Istria towns (see www.zigantetartufi.com), and the Zigante restaurant in Livade *(see p.53)*.

SOUVENIRS

Handicrafts

Craftsmanship is highly valued in Croatia, and many souvenirs are still made by hand.

In Istria you might like to buy a *bukaleta*, a traditional wooden mug for drinking wine, which can be found in souvenir shops in Poreč and Rovinj. Here you will also find ceramic models of *kašuni*, the round stone huts seen in this region.

In the south you can buy replicas of traditional Dalmatian stone houses. The best place to shop for handmade gifts in Split is in the podrum, the underground gallery leading from the seafront to the peristyle. Dubrovnik was renowned for its gold- and silver-smiths, and today filigree jewellery is a speciality. A number of jewellers around Od Puca sell modern as well as old and antique pieces.

If visiting Zagorje and the Zagreb area, you can buy a *licitarsko srce*, a gingerbread heart decorated with icing and a ribbon. Years ago, men would give these to the girl they loved on Valentine's Day. You will find shops selling these gifts in Zagreb, close to Trg bana Josipa Jelačića, and also in Kumrovec, Zagorje.

Natural Products

You can pick up sponges at reasonable prices in souvenir shops in Šibenik. They come from the nearby island of Krapanj, where they have been the main source of income for generations.

Visitors to the island of Hvar will be struck by the lavender-scented air. In the summer you can buy dried lavender and lavender perfume from all main tourist centres.

Alternatively, take home the summer fragrances of the Dalmatian islands by shopping at Aromatica (www.aromatica.hr), which produces herbal soaps, natural skin creams, massage oils and teas, and has shops in Zagreb (Vlaška 7) and Rovinj (Carera 33).

Above from far left: basket-weaving; sponges from Krapanj; gingerbread heart; elegant Oktogon shopping arcade in Zagreb.

Below: dried lavender from Hvar.

Markets

Wherever you go, allow some time to visit the local open-air market, where you will find a colourful array of stalls laden with seasonal fruit and vegetables that are bursting with taste. Honey is not the easiest thing to pack in your suitcase, but you may well be tempted to buy some from beekeepers who display their produce on small wooden stands. Slightly more manageable while travelling are non-perishable goods: look out for dried figs, walnuts, strings of garlic and bunches of dried hot red peppers. Herbal teas are popular for therapeutic purposes; there seems to be one for every ailment. Markets invariably feature an elderly lady bartering bags of sun-dried *šipak* (rosehip), *kamomil* (camomile), *menta* (mint) and *kadulja* (sage), all of which are far more flavoursome than the pre-packed varieties. Food markets tend only to be open in the mornings.

ENTERTAINMENT

Culturally, there is plenty going on in Croatia. Music-lovers are particularly well catered for; there are festivals aplenty, plus a full programme of classical concerts in major cities and Croatian pop. Jazz is growing in popularity, and nightclubs spin all the latest sounds.

THE ARTS

Concerts, opera and plays offer excellent value for money, as tickets are relatively cheap and the quality is high. Croatians became used to government subsidies for the arts under the Yugoslav regime, and still expect to have their tastes satisfied at a relatively low cost. They take pride in supporting Croatian composers and musicians, even though few have attained international renown.

Zagreb, Split and Dubrovnik are the major cultural centres where you can hear first-rate musicians and singers perform. Zagreb has its own opera, theatre and ballet company (check www.hnk.hr for schedules), and the major concert hall is the Vatroslav Lisinski (www.lisinski.hr; *see p.122*). Dubrovnik even has its own symphony orchestra, which is a remarkable show of support for the arts considering the size of the town (see www.dso.hr). The concert, ballet and opera season runs from October until May, which is another good reason to come to Croatia off-season.

CINEMA

Croatia has a burgeoning cinema scene, although foreign blockbusters tend to crowd out Croatian films in local cinemas. Foreign films are always shown in the original language with subtitles. In the summer, many resorts offer open-air cinema, with projections commencing after sunset.

CROATIAN MUSIC

While enjoying international pop hits, Croatians have a massive appreciation of their own musical heritage. One of the most popular forms of folk music is *klapa*, when a group of men or women sing a cappella in harmony. The music is haunting and expressive. You

Below: the Moreška sword dance has been a tradition of Korčula since the 15th century *(see margin, p.94).*

do not need to understand the words in order to be affected by the themes of love (often for the homeland) and loss. *Klapa* is particularly popular in Dalmatia and it is not confined to professional performances; the songs are widely known, and sung whenever a group of people is in the mood.

Croatian pop stars enjoy a huge following at home and throughout the former Yugoslavia. Tereza Kesovija, Oliver Dragojević, Severina and Gibonni are some of the artists whose music is frequently on the radio. It is worth checking out their concerts. To see up-and-coming stars, try to catch the Split Music Festival in July. Croatian music companies use the festival as a venue to introduce new artists, and at least one new summer hit comes out of the festival each year.

FESTIVALS

July and August are replete with music festivals. The most prestigious is the Dubrovnik Summer Festival (www.dubrovnik-festival.hr), which attracts artists – particularly classical musicians and actors – of the highest calibre. Medieval palaces, fortresses and courtyards provide delightful backdrops to the outdoor performances. It is also a good time to catch an off-season concert by the Dubrovnik Symphony Orchestra, and there are also plenty of visiting orchestras and soloists from around Europe. The programme includes top-notch folk performances, too. One perennial favourite is the Lado Ensemble of Zagreb, composed of

highly accomplished singers and dancers versed in the Croatian folk tradition.

Another great summer event is the Split Summer Festival (www.splitsko-ljeto.hr), which presents a variety of concerts, plays and exhibitions around town. Open-air opera on the peristyle is the main attraction, with a Verdi opera always topping the bill.

Istria also has its culture-fests. June sees Music Evenings in Grožnjan, with Grožnjan Music Summer School concerts through to August. In nearby Motovun, a film festival is held in late July (www.motovunfilmfestival.com). The Pula Summer Festival is more pop-oriented, with an emphasis on Croatian entertainers. The festival venue is Pula's Roman amphitheatre, which is also frequently the site of shows throughout the year (www.histriafestival.com).

Poreč hosts jazz concerts in the courtyard of the Baroque Sinčić Palace in June and July, and the Basilica of St Euphrasius holds classical recitals from June to September.

NIGHTCLUBS

The wildest and most varied nightlife is found in Zagreb, which has everything from jazz clubs to mega-discos. In summer the scene travels to the coast and islands. The summer nightlife capital is trendy Hvar Town with its chic clubs, but there are also vast open-air discos in Split and on Pag Island. Pula has the most popular nightlife in Istria, often based on Verudela peninsula. For nightlife and entertainment listings, *see pp.122–3*.

Above from far left: folk performance in the Rector's Palace, Dubrovnik; Aquarius nightclub, Zagreb.

Summer Nights
For most of the summer season, it is easy to become acquainted with Croatian folk dancers and singers, as the most popular groups tour the coast and islands, usually performing for free in the town square in the early evening. Later the music shifts to the terraces of the large hotels, where local groups play international standards. The casual atmosphere makes it a good family event. As a rule, the better the hotel, the better the music.

OUTDOOR ACTIVITIES

Scuba-diving, sailing, windsurfing and swimming in the coastal waters attract most visitors, but Croatia's interior also provides an armful of opportunities to get physical, with hiking, rock-climbing and cycling.

Naturism
Naturism has a long and venerable history in Croatia, even though Croatians seldom bare all at the beach. The largest naturist resort is Koversada in Istria, but there are secluded coves and bays for naturists all along the Croatian littoral. Look for the sign *FKK*, which signifies a naturist beach.

Below: kayaking is a good way to explore the coast.

Of course you could simply relax on a beach and take occasional dips in the sea, but if you have a more active holiday in mind Croatia offers a wealth of choice. Croatians are very outdoors-oriented and take full advantage of their mountains and sea, so participating in an activity is also a good way to meet locals. Tourist offices will have detailed information on sporting associations, equipment rental and routes.

CLIMBING

The karstic stone of Croatia's coastline is great for climbers. The caves and canyons of Paklenica National Park, near Zadar, make up one of the most important climbing sites in the country, popular with climbers at all levels. Con-

tact the Visitors' Centre (tel: 023-369 155; www.paklenica.hr). Other climbing sites include Biokovo Nature Park *(see margin, p.63)* and Marjan hill, Split.

CYCLING

In summer you can hire mountain bikes in all the main tourist centres. Central Istria has a number of well-maintained cycle paths; the Istria Tourist Board produces a comprehensive map of cycling routes, including distances, time, altitude and difficulty (www.istria-bike.com). The disused Trieste-Poreč railway track (the Parenzana) hosts an annual four-day cycle and mountain-bike event (www.parenzana.com).

Hvar has allocated a number of minor roads and tracks to mountain biking; the tourist office has details. Mljet's excellent cycle paths run through the national park's dense forests and around the lakes.

DIVING

More thrills await underwater. Scuba-diving is superb along the Croatian coast, and there are dive centres on nearly every island and in most coastal towns. The primary dive highlights are caves and shipwrecks. The caves are a

feature of Croatia's karstic rock, and the shipwrecks are a result of the powerful navies that once fought for dominance of the Adriatic. The most famous shipwreck is the *Baron Gautsch* near Rovinj *(see feature, p.47)* but there are plenty of others. Vis Island is known for its waters that teem with fish, as the island was off-limits for many years *(see p.68)*. For more details see the National Tourist Board's diving pages (www.croatia.hr).

HIKING

The Dinaric mountains running parallel to the coast are a popular destination for hikers. There are a number of mountain huts, especially in the Velebit range north of Zadar, that provide simple but adequate lodging; it is wise to reserve in advance on summer weekends. Hiking paths are marked with a white dot within a red circle, but in more remote areas the markings have worn away or been removed by shepherds. The best hiking spot in southern Dalmatia is Biokovo Mountain *(see margin, p.63)*. If you start early, you can make it to the top of the 1,762m (5,778ft) Sveti Jure peak in one day. Biokovo Active Holidays (tel: 021-679 655; www.biokovo.net) organises guided hikes in central Dalmatia. Hvar Island is a good choice for easier walks *(see margin, right)*.

SAILING

Croatia truly is a sailor's paradise; indeed, the best way to appreciate its islands is by boat, as you can explore those that are inaccessible by ferry. Most of the islands mentioned in this book have agencies that rent out small motorboats for the day, but you may want to see more. Those without sailing experience can opt for a skippered boat, but those with nautical experience can go 'bareboat' (you will need to produce a valid recreational boat licence as well as a radio certificate). Contact the Adriatic Club International (ACI), whose head office is in Opatija (tel: 052-271 288; www.aci-club.hr).

SWIMMING

For those who enjoy swimming in the sea, the Adriatic is a dream. From Istria to Dubrovnik, there is nothing but clean water with average temperatures of 23–26°C (73–79°F) in summer. The water can stay warm enough for swimming until October. There are so many sheltered coves that currents are rarely a problem, and the only dangerous sea creatures are urchins. Few beaches are sandy, however, and some are quite rocky.

WINDSURFING

The most popular windsurfing site in Croatia, for those visitors who are really serious about their sport, is at Bol, on Brač Island *(see margin, p.60)*, where the winds are reliably good from May to October. Viganj, in the southwest of the Pelješac peninsula *(see pp.90–1)*, and the Premantura peninsula outside Pula, are also good windsurfing areas. For more information, check www.windsurfing.hr and www.orca-sport.com.

Above from far left: yachts on Vis Island; rock-climbing in Paklenica National Park; cycling on Hvar.

Hiking on Hvar
Hvar Island *(see p.72)* offers gentler hikes, perfect for the warm summer season or for casual hikers. Hvar Adventure (tel: 091-154 3072; www.hvaradventure.com) organises a number of hiking tours to various beautiful and remote island destinations. Be sure to come equipped with strong, ankle-high walking boots: the jagged rocks can be treacherous on Hvar and other islands.

HISTORY: KEY DATES

Croatian history, both ancient and modern, is characterised by turbulence. Over the years, invading armies gobbled up territory only to be pushed out by other armies. All were vying for the fertile interior and the long coastline that was so essential for commercial and military control of the Adriatic.

EARLY PERIOD

1000BC	Illyrians arrive on Balkan peninsula.
4th century BC	First Greek colonies are founded on Adriatic islands, notably Issa on Vis.
1st century BC	Romans arrive in Dalmatia and Istria, and found coastal settlements. Interior remains inhabited by Illyrians.
395AD	Roman territory is divided into Western and Eastern empires.
555	Istrian and Dalmatian coast become part of Byzantine Empire.
7th century	Slavs arrive on Balkan peninsula.
925	King Tomislav unites Dalmatia and Pannonia to form what is today roughly the territory of Croatia.
1054	Christian Church is divided between Rome and Constantinople.

RISE OF EMPIRES

1091	Croatia signs Pacta Conventa, recognising Hungarian royalty in return for self-government under a viceroy.
1240	Tatar invasion of Central Europe; destruction throughout Croatia.
1358	Birth of Republic of Ragusa (Dubrovnik).
1420	Venice takes Istrian and Dalmatian coasts.
16th century	Turks take Slavonia, Dalmatian hinterland and unprotected coastal towns. Austria develops Krajina military border.
1699	Croatia is liberated from Turkish rule. The Habsburgs take Pannonia, Venice takes Dalmatia; only Dubrovnik is independent.

AUSTRO-HUNGARIAN RULE

1797	Venetian Republic ends. Dalmatia and Istria come under Austro-Hungarian control.
1805	Napoleon unites Dalmatia, Istria and much of Slovenia under the Illyrian Provinces.

1808	Republic of Dubrovnik is abolished.
1815	Fall of Napoleon. Dalmatia comes under Habsburg rule.
1881	Krajina is incorporated into Croatia.
1914	Shooting of Archduke Franz Ferdinand sparks World War I.

YUGOSLAVIA

1918	Croatia becomes part of Kingdom of Serbs, Croats and Slovenes under King Aleksandar.
1934	King Aleksandar is assassinated by extremists.
1941	Germany declares war on Yugoslavia. Ustaše seizes power in Croatia. Tito forms Partisan movement.
1945	Tito founds Federal Democratic People's Republic of Yugoslavia with Croatia as one of the six republics.
1971	'Croatian Spring' fuels nationalist fervour. Agitators imprisoned.
1980	Tito dies. Yugoslavia is left with a system of rotating presidency.
1980s	Economic crisis sets in. Slovenia and Croatia object to funding poorer republics. Milošević assumes power in Belgrade as Serbian nationalism grows.
1990	Franjo Tudjman is elected president as his Croatian Democratic Union (HDZ) wins elections on nationalist manifesto.

WAR AND PEACE

1991	Croatia proclaims independence; Serb population proclaims Republic of Serbian Krajina, blockading a third of Croatia. War breaks out. Croats in Vukovar are among the worst casualties.
1992	EU and UN recognise Croatia. UN peacekeepers deployed to oversee ceasefire and protect Serb minority.
1995	Croats take back Serb-held areas of Slavonia and Krajina – thousands of Serbs have no choice but to leave.
1999	President Tudjman dies.

TOWARDS THE EU

2004	Croatia becomes an official candidate for EU membership.
2005	Former General Ante Gotovina is arrested and brought to The Hague to face trial for war crimes committed in expelling the Krajina Serbs.
2008	Croatia settles dispute with Italy and Slovenia over Adriatic fishing rights, removing final obstacle to EU membership.

WALKS AND TOURS

ZAGREB: UPPER TOWN

Stroll through Zagreb's Upper Town (Gornji grad), the oldest part of Croatia's capital city, with a look at the cathedral, the local market, historic monuments and the city's most appealing cafés.

DISTANCE 2km (1 mile)
TIME A half day; a full day with museum visits
START Trg Bana Josipa Jelačića
END Lotrščak Tower
POINTS TO NOTE

Do this tour in the morning to get the full flavour of Dolac and to arrive at Lotrščak Tower at noon in time for the firing of the cannon. It can then be combined with the tour of the Lower Town *(see pp.30–3)* in the afternoon.

Below: keeping watch over the cathedral.

Street Names

There are two ways of rendering street names in Zagreb: in either the nominative or possessive case. So, Ulica Ivana Tkalčića (street of Ivan Tkalčić) becomes Tkalčićeva ulica (Tkalčić's street). Usually, the former is how the name is written on street signs, while the latter is how the street names are shown on maps and are spoken. Thus there may be a slight difference between the street names in this book, the street names on maps and the names on the streets themselves.

Food and Drink 🍴

① GRADSKA KAVANA
Trg Bana Josipa Jelačića 9; tel: 01-481 3005; daily 7.30am–10.30pm; €
This stately old coffee house is a Zagreb classic, populated by a stable of regulars who settle in for coffee to animate their political discussions.

② IVICA I MARICA
Tkalčićeva 70; tel: 01-481 7321; www.ivicaimarica.com; Mon–Sat 10am–11pm, Sun 9am–10pm; €
Known for their meltingly delicious cakes (free of artificial additives and preservatives), Ivica and Marica have expanded their offerings. You can now try a range of Zagreb specialities such as *štrukli* (a type of curd cheese dough dumplings) and a selection of vegetarian dishes.

The history of Zagreb's Upper Town (Gornji grad) is a tale of two hilltop cities: Gradec and Kaptol. Kaptol was under the jurisdiction of the Church, while Gradec was under the direct control of the reigning monarch from the 13th to 17th centuries. Even now, Kaptol has a more sober look than leafy Gradec. The encroachment of the Turks in the 16th century forced the two communities to merge, but the new city was beset by fire and plague which sent the economy into a tailspin. In the 19th century rail links put Zagreb at the crossroads of the Austro-Hungarian Empire; it grew prosperous, developing a flourishing cultural and intellectual life, and entered its Golden Age.

Zagreb took a back seat to Belgrade during the Yugoslav years, but has now re-established itself as one of Eastern Europe's most exciting cities, with world-class shopping, superb dining and a vibrant artistic scene.

KAPTOL

You could begin the morning with coffee at **Gradska Kavana**, see 🍴①, on **Trg Bana Josipa Jelačića ❶**.

Cathedral

Leave the square by the passage in the northeast corner in the direction of the

church spires. Walk uphill about 50m/ yds on Bakačeva until you reach, on the right, the **Cathedral of the Assumption of the Virgin Mary ❷** (Katedrala Marijina Uznesenja; 7am–7.30pm; free) in the heart of Kaptol. The original building dates from the 12th century, but the neo-Gothic façade and twin bell towers were added by Viennese architect Herman Bollé in the 19th century. Step inside to see a medieval inscription of the Ten Commandments on the north wall. It is written in Glagolitic script, which dates from the 9th century and was devised to translate the Bible *(see p.52)*. Also on the north wall is the tomb of Cardinal Stepinac, carved by Ivan Meštrović *(see p.28 and p.58)*. Stepinac was the archbishop of Zagreb during World War II. He was beatified despite controversy surrounding his role under the Nazi puppet regime.

Walk north up Kaptol to Opatovina on the left and follow the street downhill past the cosy cafés and bars. The street traces the line of the former walls that once surrounded Kaptol.

Belly of Zagreb

At the end of Opatovina is **Dolac ❸** (Mon–Fri 7am–4pm, Sat–Sun 7am– 2pm), the market known as the 'Belly of Zagreb', which opened in 1926. A number of colourful fruit and vegetable stalls occupy the open-air upper level, while directly below, an impeccable indoor market deals in dairy products, salamis, home-cured hams and a sumptuous array of breads and cakes. After a snack, leave Dolac by Tkalčićeva, one street west of Opatovina.

Café Culture

Tkalčićeva ❹ was once a waterway that formed the natural boundary between Gradec and Kaptol. A stream flowed here, powering several mills, until 1898, when it was filled in and a street built over it. Tkalčićeva is now the pulse of Zagreb café life, a busy pedestrian zone lined with restaurants, bars and cafés with outdoor seating. Stop here for a *palačinke* (pancake) at **Ivica I Marica**, see ⑪②.

GRADEC

Turn left on Mlinarske stube and go up the steep wooden steps to Radićeva. Turn left and a short way down, on the right side of the street, is the pretty **Stone Gate ❺** (Kamenita vrata), once the gate to Gradec. The original 13th-century town walls had four gates, of which only the Stone Gate remains.

Above from far left: view of the Upper Town from the Lower Town; nun entering the cathedral; plums at the Dolac market; Glagolitic script in the cathedral.

Below: one of Dolac market's distinctive red umbrellas; chestnuts for sale.

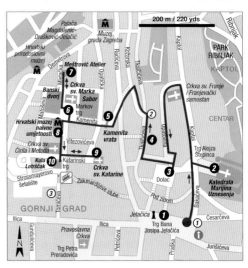

Miraculous Virgin

According to local legend, a terrible fire broke out at the site of the Stone Gate in 1731 and all the surrounding wooden buildings were razed to the ground. Hidden in the ashes, only one thing remained; a picture of the Virgin Mary, miraculously intact. The Stone Gate thus became a shrine of miracles, where people light a candle and pray. If their prayer is answered they pay tribute to the Virgin with a plaque. Supplication seems to work here: the walls are covered with small marble tablets engraved with *hvala* (thank you).

Within the arched gateway stands an enchanting shrine to the Virgin Mary, full of flowers and flickering candles *(see margin, left)*.

St Mark's Square

Leave the gate on the other side at Kamenita ulica. Follow it to **Markov trg ❻**, crowned by **St Mark's Church** (Crkva sv. Marka), with its extraordinary coloured roof. In contrast to St Catherine's *(see p.29)*, this church was erected as a humble place of prayer for the craftsmen of Gradec in the 13th century. In the 19th century the church was subject to extensive reconstruction work, part of which gave it the Hungarian-style roof. The emblem on the roof's right is that of the city of Zagreb. The emblem to the left represents the coat of arms of Croatia, Dalmatia and Slavonia, which originally made up the medieval kingdom.

The nation's governmental and administrative buildings are clustered around Markov trg, hence the low-key police presence. On the eastern side of the square, behind the church, stands the **Parliament building** (Sabor), and on the western side, opposite the church

entrance, stands the **Ban's Palace** (Banski dvori), the seat of the Croatian government. The peasant revolutionary Matija Gubec was executed in this square in 1573, following a failed peasant uprising. The stone face carved on the corner building between Ćirilometodska ulica and Kamenita ulica is assumed to be a monument to Gubec.

Meštrović Atelier

Pass through the square to the north to find Mletačka. At no. 8 stands the beautiful **Meštrović Atelier ❼** (tel: 01-485 1123; www.mdc.hr/mestrovic; Mon–Fri 10am–6pm, Sat–Sun 10am–2pm; charge). Often unjustly neglected by the international art world, Ivan Meštrović (1883–1962) deserves a place in the pantheon of the greatest sculptors of the 20th century. More than 100 figurative works, in wood, bronze and marble, are arranged informally throughout the artist's former home, studio and garden.

Croatian Museum of Naïve Art

Return to Markov trg and take Ćirilometodska on the opposite (southern) side to reach the **Croatian Museum of Naïve Art ❽** (Hrvatski muzej naivne umjetnosti; tel: 01-485 1911; www.hmnu.org; Tue–Fri 10am–6pm, Sat–Sun 10am–1pm; charge) at no. 3. Unique to Croatia, this movement was founded in the 1930s by a group of peasants with no formal artistic education. Their works portray scenes from rural life, employing peculiar perspectives and garish colours. More recent Naïve painters are also represented.

Food and Drink 🍴
③ VALLIS AUREA
Tomićeva 4; tel: 01-483 1305;
Mon–Sat 9am–11pm; €€
This cosy restaurant highlights the food and wine of the Slavonia region of eastern Croatia, known for its wine, sausage and paprika-laced dishes. From smoked ribs to trout, the hearty fare never disappoints.

St Catherine's Church

At the end of Ćirilometodska is Katarinski trg. Turn left here and you will find the Baroque **St Catherine's Church** ❾ (Crkva sv. Katarine; opening times vary; free). This church, which was built by Jesuit monks in the early 17th century, is considered one of the most beautiful pieces of Baroque architecture in the country. Decorated to flatter the local aristocracy of that time, the interior is encrusted with sugary pink-and-white stucco-work that resembles icing on a cake. Be sure not to miss the extremely deceptive fresco above the altar.

Lotrščak Tower

Cross Katarinski trg, then take the short street of Dverce and you will arrive at **Lotrščak Tower** ❿ (Kula Lotrščak). Dating back to 1266, this is the best-preserved part of the city's 13th-century fortifications. It originally protected the southern entrance to Gradec, and every evening a bell would ring to signal the closing of the town gates. As the centuries passed and the likelihood of outside attack waned, the tower became a firefighters' lookout. These days it is the home of the **Galerija Lotrščak** (Tue–Sun 11am–7pm). Art exhibitions are held here, although many people enter only to climb the tower for a panoramic view of the city.

Every day at noon the **city cannon** is fired from the tower. The tradition began in 1877 when a daily, highly audible 'bang' was considered the most foolproof way of synchronising the haphazardly timed chimes of the city's countless church bells. Today, compressed paper and cardboard explode from the barrel with a mighty blast, and local children gather below the tower to collect the shreds.

The Lotrščak Tower marks the beginning of **Strossmayerovo šetalište**, which has magnificent views over Zagreb's rooftops and domes. From here you can take the **funicular** down to Tomićeva and enjoy a big lunch at **Vallis Aurea**, see ⓸③.

Above from far left: a glimpse of St Mark's Church roof; façades on Radićeva; Lotrščak Tower; funicular to the Lower Town.

Zagreb Nightlife

Let it not be said that Zagreb is staid or behind the times when it comes to after-dark fun. Upper Town, Lower Town and out-of-town all have their venues. The centre of Upper Town nightlife is Tkalčićeva, with its rows of bars, pubs and cafés. Here you bar-hop and hang out. The Lower Town is where to go for live music. BP Club (Teslina 7; www.bpclub.hr) and Sax (Palmotićeva 22; www.sax-zg.hr) handle the jazz, while Kset (Unska 3; www.kset.org) presents an eclectic assortment of contemporary sounds. Because Jarun Lake is several kilometres southwest of the town centre, no one minds the vast discos installed on its shores. Aquarius is the current favourite. For details of Aquarius and more nightlife listings, *see p.122.*

ZAGREB: LOWER TOWN

This walking tour takes you through the 'green horseshoe', the necklace of parks and gardens that nearly encloses Zagreb's commercial and cultural heart in the Lower Town (Donji grad).

DISTANCE 3.5km (2¼ miles)
TIME A half day; a full day with museum visits
START/END Trg Bana Josipa Jelačića
POINTS TO NOTE
On Mondays most museums are closed. You could pick up a Zagreb Card (see p.33) at the tourist office to economise on admission fees.

Laid out from 1865 to 1887, Zagreb's 'green horseshoe' was intended to bring architecture and greenery into harmony. Most of Zagreb's cultural monuments are displayed along this verdant swathe that runs from the interconnected concrete garden squares of Trg maršala Tita, Mažuranićev trg and Marulićev trg, across the Botanical Gardens and up the east side from Tomislavov trg, Strossmayerov trg and Zrinjevac to Trg Bana Josipa Jelačića.

Croata Cravata

Croatia is the homeland of the necktie, but don't hold it against them! The earliest version was more like a scarf than today's knotted fabric, but the new style soon became all the rage in 17th-century Paris. Croata Cravata (Oktogon; tel: 01-481 2726; Mon–Sat 8.30am–6pm) is the best place to buy the highest-quality silk neckties or, for ladies, colourful silk scarves.

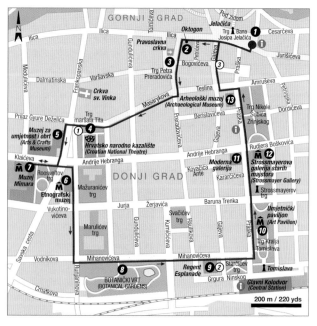

TRG BANA JOSIPA JELAČIĆA

If you are starting from the end point of tour 1, turn left at Ilica and proceed to Oktogon on the right. Otherwise, begin at **Trg Bana Josipa Jelačića ❶**, Zagreb's central square that acts as the boundary between the Upper and Lower towns. In the middle of the square stands an imposing statue of *ban* (viceroy) Jelačić upon a horse. Following the orientation of the statue, turn right off the square into Ilica, the city's main shopping street, lined with boutiques.

Stay on the left side of the street and in about 200m/yds, you will come to the wrought-iron gates of the **Oktogon ❷**, a late 19th-century shopping arcade full of upmarket boutiques and topped by a stained-glass dome.

Trg Petra Preradovića

Pass through the eight-cornered structure and on the other side is **Trg Petra Preradovića ❸**. Petar Preradović (1818–72), after whom the square was named, was a general and Romantic poet. You can see his memorial statue in front of the **Orthodox Church** (Pravoslavna crkva). This square is also called **Cvijetni trg** (Field of the Flowers); it was once the site of a big flower market, although today only a few flower sellers set up stalls here every day.

TRG MARŠALA TITA

From Preradovićeva trg, proceed south along Preradovićeva ulica, then take the first right to follow Masarykova to **Trg maršala Tita ❹** (Marshal Tito Square), the first of a series of three squares that make up one side of the green horseshoe and undoubtedly the most monumental piazza in Zagreb, laid out by 19th-century Viennese architect Herman Bollé. The central building here is the neo-Baroque **National Theatre** (Hrvatsko narodno kazalište), completed in a record 14 months to be ready for the visit of Emperor Franz Joseph in 1895. The theatre, along with the other buildings intended to host entertainment and the arts, was painted in 'royal and imperial yellow'.

In front of the theatre is Ivan Meštrović's *(see p.28)* enchanting **Well of Life Fountain** (Zdenac života).

Above from far left: statue of Ban Jelačić; neo-Baroque National Theatre; reading in Zagreb's central square; National Theatre at night.

Below: park within Zagreb's green horseshoe.

Statue of Josip Jelačić

Ban Josip Jelačić was one of Croatia's most beloved heroes. As *ban* (viceroy), he agitated, unsuccessfully, for greater autonomy for Croatia within the Austrian Empire. Ironically, it was a Viennese sculptor, Antun Fernkorn, who erected the monument to him in Trg Bana Josipa Jelačića in 1866. The monument and square quickly became a focal point for Croatian nationalist aspirations, which is why Tito had the statue removed and the square renamed Trg Republike when he came to power in 1945.

When dreams of an independent Croatia resurfaced in 1989, restoration of the Jelačić statue and square became a rallying cry for the new nationalism. Petitions were organised, donations collected and the statue was reassembled after 43 years in a basement. President Tudjman, known for his love of pomp and ceremony, unveiled the statue at night, amidst a triumphant display of fireworks. A popular Zagreb meeting point is 'under the tail' of the statue: should you have a rendezvous to keep in the city centre, this is the place to do it.

Below: details from the Museum of Arts and Crafts.

While still a student in Vienna, the sculptor designed a prototype that featured in an exhibition of works by members of the Vienna Secession movement in 1906. The bronze fountain that you see here was installed in 1912.

On the western side of the square at no. 10 stands the **Museum of Arts and Crafts ❺** (Muzej za umjetnost i obrt; tel: 01-488 2110; www.muo.hr; Tue, Wed–Sat 10am–7pm (Thur to 10pm), Sun 10am–2pm; charge), also designed by Bollé. Inside is a vast collection of furniture and decorative arts dating from medieval times to the present day. Among the many religious works, the 17th-century altar of St Mary on the first floor is a standout.

Before leaving the square you could stop for a break at fashionable **Hemingway Bar**, see Ⓨ①.

Ethnographic Museum

Proceed south to the adjacent square, Mažuranićev trg, and on your right at no. 14 is the **Ethnographic Museum ❻** (Etnografski muzej; tel: 01-482 6220; www.etnografski-musej.hr; Tue–Thur 10am–6pm, Fri–Sun 10am–1pm; charge). The museum is housed in a monumental 1903 edifice and honours Croatian folk history by showcasing traditional costumes, jewellery and handicrafts. The surprising array of objects from the South Pacific, Asia and South America were amassed by early 20th-century Croatian explorers Mirko and Stevo Seljan.

Mimara Museum

Heading west across the busy Savska cesta, you will come to Roosveltov trg. Here, at no. 5, a massive grey neo-Renaissance building houses the **Mimara Museum ❼** (Muzej Mimara; tel: 01-482 8100; www.mimara.hr; Tue–Sat 10am–5pm, Thur until 7pm; charge), containing priceless and eclectic collections of artefacts, including Chinese porcelain, and paintings by Flemish and Spanish masters. The museum's founder, Ante Topić Mimara (1898–1987), is something of mystery. He spent most of his life abroad, and no one has managed to explain the source of his extraordinary wealth. Towards the end of his life he donated his entire art collection to the city of Zagreb.

Food and Drink 🍴

① HEMINGWAY BAR
Tuškanac 1; tel: 01-483 4956/5; www.hemingway.hr; daily 10am–midnight; €
This immensely trendy café-cocktail bar is open all day for coffee and cakes but really takes off at night. Pictures of the 'bearded one' adorn the walls while bartenders mix up Zagreb's most elaborate cocktails. At night smarter attire is expected.

② ZINFANDEL'S
Regent Esplanade hotel, Mihanovićeva 1; tel: 01-456 6666; www.zinfandels.com.hr; daily noon–11pm; €€–€€€
A superb hotel deserves a superb restaurant, and Zinfandel's is definitely it. Chef Marc Fontenelle fuses contemporary flavours with Balkan specialities to wonderful effect, and a lower-priced Bistro also offers more casual fare. In either venue, the *štrukli (see p.15)* are a must, either as a starter, a dessert or a snack.

③ BOBAN
Gajeva 9; tel: 01-481 1549; daily 10am–midnight; €
At Boban, you can choose to eat in the café-lounge-bar upstairs or the downstairs restaurant. In nice weather, people cluster around the outdoor tables. Select one of the imaginative pasta dishes from the tempting restaurant menu, and be prepared to wait.

BOTANICAL GARDENS

Return to Mažuranićev trg, head south to Marulićev trg, then turn left into Mihanovićeva. On the opposite side of the road lie the beautiful **Botanical Gardens ❽** (Botanički vrt; www. botanic.hr; daily, check website for opening hours; free), which offer respite from the hustle of the city.

Proceed east along Mihanovićeva to the **Regent Esplanade hotel ❾** *(see p.109)*. Built in 1925, this illustrious building was originally intended to provide an overnight stop for passengers of the once-popular Orient Express, hence the proximity to the **Central Station** (Glavni Kolodvor). You may wish to stop for lunch in the Esplanade's elegant restaurant, **Zinfandel's**, see ⑪②.

AROUND TRG KRALJA TOMISLAVA

Continue east, passing the equestrian statue of King Tomislav in front of the Central Station. It was Tomislav who drew up a definitive map of Croatian territory in 925AD. Turn left onto Praška and the leafy **Trg Kralja Tomislava** (King Tomislav Square) will be on your right. Continue until you reach the **Art Pavilion ❿** (Umjetnički paviljon; Mon–Sat 11am–7pm, Sun 10am–1pm; www.umjetnicki-paviljon.hr; charge) at its centre. Standing out against its verdant backdrop, the striking yellow Art Nouveau structure was erected to celebrate '1,000 years of Hungarian Culture' in Budapest in 1896, and now presents changing contemporary art exhibitions.

Modern Art and Old Masters

Continue along Praška with **Strossmayerov trg**, another shady park, on your right. On your left is the **Gallery of Modern Art ⓫** (Moderna galerija; tel: 01-492 2368; Tue–Fri 10am–6pm, Sat–Sun 10am–1pm; charge), which is an essential stop for anyone interested in modern Croatian art. All the Croatian masters, from Vlaho Bukovac to Milan Račić, are represented here.

On your right, housed in the **Croatian Academy of Arts and Sciences**, is the **Strossmayer Gallery of Old Masters ⓬** (Strossmayerova galerija starih majstora; tel: 01-481 3344; www.mdc. hr/strossmayer; Tue 10am–1pm and 5–7pm, Wed–Sun 10am–1pm; charge), which represents the collection of Bishop Strossmayer, donated in 1884. The cultivated bishop and advocate for Croatian autonomy amassed artwork from the four corners of Europe. Bellini, El Greco and Van Dyck are some of the great masters on display.

Archaeological Museum

Continue along Praška to Trg Nikole Šubića Zrinjskog, the square at the end of the horseshoe. On your left is the **Archaeological Museum ⓭** (Arheološki muzej; tel: 01-487 3101; www. amz.hr; Tue–Fri 10am–5pm, Thur until 8pm, Sat–Sun 10am–1pm; charge), most famous for its Egyptian mummy. There are also prehistoric and medieval artefacts, plus the largest coin collection in Europe. Turn left at Teslina and right at Gajeva, where you can take a break at **Boban**, see ⑪③. Trg Bana Josipa Jelačića is just to the north.

Above from far left: Botanical Gardens scene and turtle; exhibit inside the Art Pavilion; Gallery of Modern Art.

Zagreb Card
Visiting multiple museums? It may pay to invest in the Zagreb Card. For 60Kn you get unlimited tram travel plus free or reduced admission to dozens of museums and sights. You can even get discounts in some shops and restaurants. You can buy them online (www.zagrebcard. fivestars.hr) or at the tourist office at Trg Bana Jelačića 11.

ZAGORJE

Escape from the bustle of Zagreb to the hills of Zagorje, which lie to the north of the capital. This is a land of farmhouses, castles and medieval fortresses, with Staro Selo – the birthplace of Tito and now a fascinating open-air ethnographic museum – a star attraction.

DISTANCE 170km (106 miles)
TIME A full day
START/END Zagreb
POINTS TO NOTE

This itinerary requires a car, as neither Veliki Tabor nor Trakošćan can be reached by public transport (although it is possible to do a half-day trip from Zagreb to Kumrovec by local train, changing at Savski Mariof). Make an early start, and time it to arrive in Grešna Gorica for lunch.

The undulating farmland, vineyards and rural villages of the Croatian hinterland, **Zagorje**, lie less than an hour north of Zagreb. Unlike the Mediterranean style of the coast, the cool hills, hearty cuisine and German-speaking inhabitants leave you in no doubt that you are in Eastern Europe.

To get to the region, leave Zagreb via Zagorska magistrala (Route 225), the former main road to Ljubljana, which runs parallel to the E59/A2 motorway. Although not the quickest route, it is the more interesting one.

INTO THE HILLS

After driving for around 15km (10 miles), head west to Luka then head north. After 5km (3¼ miles) you will pass through the village of **Veliko Trgovišće ❶**, the birthplace of the late President Tudjman. You cannot miss the house; a single-storey, green-and-white affair on the corner, to your right, with a chequered Croatian flag in the garden and a memorial plaque. Tudjman, it seems, hoped to be immortalised in the way Tito was.

After the village take a route north through the rolling hills until you reach Route 205. Note the vineyards planted in narrow strips running vertically down the slopes, each with its own small wooden hut *(klet)*, that was traditionally used for storing wine. Villages in the area like Družilovec and Dubrovčan are typical rural settlements with steep tiled roofs, open-sided wooden barns filled with maize, and ducks and geese waddling along the roadside.

Food and Drink

① ZAGORSKA KLET

Musej Staro Selo; tel: 049-553 107; www.mdc.hr/kumrovec;
summer 9am–7pm, winter 9am–4pm; €–€€
The restaurant here serves well-prepared traditional Zagorjan dishes such as *štrukli* (a type of cheese dumpling) and *mlinci* (baked noodles), but as it caters exclusively to tourists there is a predictable impact on the prices. It is best just to stop for a drink and a snack: enough to tide you over until Grešna Gorica.

KLANJEC

Once on Route 205 travel west until you reach **Klanjec ❷** on the River Sutla. Although dominated by the imposing **Franciscan Monastery**, Klanjec is most notable as the birthplace of the sculptor Antun Augustinčić (1900–79), who created the *Monument to Peace* in front of the United Nations headquarters in New York. In the centre of town is the **Galerija** (tel: 049-550 343; www.mdc.hr/augustincic; Tue–Sun, summer 9am–5pm, winter 9am–3pm; charge), a modern museum with a striking collection of works by this remarkable artist. Notice especially the room tracing the artistic development of the *Monument to Peace* in a series of drawings and photos.

STARO SELO

Continue northwest along the River Sutla for 6km (4 miles) to **Kumrovec**, the childhood home of the Yugoslav president Josip Broz Tito. The centre of the village has been turned into the open-air ethnological museum of **Staro Selo ❸** (tel: 049-225 830; www.mdc.hr/kumrovec; daily summer 9am–7pm, winter 9am–4pm; charge). Meaning Old Village, Staro Selo comprises 20 carefully restored thatched cottages and a dozen wooden farm buildings devoted to local handicrafts and traditions. There's a blacksmith, a potter and even a gingerbread-maker, while every Sunday from May to September, visiting craftsmen give demonstrations. The simple dwellings, clustered around the stream and set amid lovingly tended gardens and orchards, paint a rather idealised picture of 19th-century rural life.

There's no doubt about which is Tito's house; a life-size statue of the man (by Augustinčić) stands in the garden. Inside, it is arranged as it would have been when Tito was a boy, with simple rustic furniture and a kitchen blackened by soot from smoking hams. People still live within the complex, but the village is more animated by farm animals. You can buy a traditional *licitarska srce* (gingerbread heart) at the souvenir shop, and you might want to stop for a drink at the **Zagorska klet** café, see ⑪①.

Bordeaux Juice
While driving, you may notice houses painted an unusual turquoise-blue colour. In the past, to protect the grapes from pests, vines were sprayed with a solution of blue copper crystals known as 'Bordeaux juice'. Any solution left over was used to paint the houses. It kept flies away during the summer months, although it is also believed to have had a detrimental effect on locals' health.

A Tragic Love Affair

Veliki Tabor is best-known for the legend of a tragic love affair between Friedrich, a nobleman, and Veronika, a beautiful local peasant girl. Freidrich's father, Count Herman, who kept court here, violently opposed the liaison. After attempting to run away together, Freidrich was imprisoned in a tower, and died, while Veronika was bricked up within the castle walls. Recent excavations here unearthed a human skeleton that allegedly is Veronika's. Perhaps the story is not simply a myth...

Miljana

On leaving Kumrovec, drive north through Zagorska Sela and Plavić. Again the road runs parallel with the River Sutla to your left, and fields and woodland to your right. You will eventually reach the 17th-century manor of **Miljana ❹**. Although it is private property, you can drive up to the gate to better admire the majestic Baroque exterior. Turn right here for Veliki Tabor and Desinić.

VELIKI TABOR

You will see the impressive fortress of **Veliki Tabor ❺** (tel: 049-343 963; www.veliki-tabor.hr; May–Sept 10am–6pm, Oct–Apr 10am–3pm; charge) perched on a hilltop just before the village of Desinić long before you arrive. Turn left, follow the track and park in front of the main gate. This is one of the area's best-preserved castles. The central core, a pentagonal tower, was built in the 12th century. The semicircular towers were added in the 15th and 16th centuries as protection against the Turks. Unfortunately, the exhibits inside – collections of tools, period weaponry, household and religious objects, paintings and pottery – fail to do justice to the imposing turrets and towers.

After exploring the fortress, return to the main road and turn left for **Desinić**. Just a few hundred metres east of the castle, you will see a sign to the right that reads, 'Seljački Turizam, **Grešna Gorica**', see ⑾②. This is a good place to stop for lunch.

TRAKOŠĆAN CASTLE

Try to finish lunch by 2.30pm, as you will need at least an hour to reach the castle at Trakošćan. Head east via Pregrada to Krapina (20km/12½ miles) At Krapina, head north onto the E59 motorway until you reach the turning east for **Trakošćan ❻** (042-796 821;

Right: hilltop castle of Trakošćan.

Food and Drink 🍽️

② GREŠNA GORICA
Desinić; tel: 049-343 001; www.gresna-gorica.com; daily 10am–10pm; €
Everything on the menu here is homemade, and all the ingredients are supplied by local farmers. Besides the hearty meat dishes that are typical of Zagorje and feature duck, pork and local venison, you might want to try *Zagorski štrukli*, a sort of maize dumpling served with fresh curd cheese. There is lots of space around this rustic restaurant, plus a playground and farmhouse zoo.

daily, www.mdc.hr/trakoscan; June–
Sept 9am–6pm, Oct–May 9am–3pm;
charge), a splendid hilltop castle. Below
are a car park, gift shop and bar.

The castle as it is seen today dates
largely from the 19th century. In 1569
the small fortress that had been here
for centuries, and its estate, were taken
by the Royal Treasury and granted to
the Bishop of Zagreb and Viceroy of
Croatia, Juraj Drašković. The bishop
treated the peasantry badly, and after
four years they rebelled. Their ring-
leader, Matija Gubec *(see p.28)* was
arrested and Drašković had him
'crowned with molten iron for his
impertinence'. The bishop handed
Trakošćan on to his brother, and it
remained in the Drašković family until
1944, when they emigrated to Austria
and the property was nationalised.

The building was uninhabited from
the 16th–19th centuries. Towards the
end of this period, when the German
Romantic movement was fashionable
among Central European aristocrats,
Trakošćan fitted the mood and sud-
denly became popular. No longer a
defence post, but a fairytale castle in
the wilderness, the building was re-
modelled in neo-Gothic style, and the
grounds landscaped on the model of an
English park. A dam was built, and the
valley turned into an artificial lake.

However, the original interior is still
intact, and it is easy to picture the
lifestyle of Zagorje nobles here. The
dark, heavy wooden furniture is complemented by solemn family portraits,
many painted by Julijana Drašković
(1847–1901).

End your visit with a walk by the
lake (full circuit, 6km/4 miles) and a
drink at the floating bar, **Terasa na
Jezeru** (May–Sept) on a raft. Sadly,
you will probably have to leave before
sunset, so you won't see the castle when
floodlit. Return to Zagreb on the E59.

Above from far left:
fortress of Veliki Tabor;
Hunting Hall at Trako-
šćan castle.

Josip Broz Tito

Josip Broz was born in Kumrovec in 1892, when Zagorje was part
of the Austro-Hungarian Empire. Taken prisoner by the Russians
during his service in World War I, he became an early convert to
Communism, and leader of the Communist party of Croatia upon
his return. When the Nazis invaded Yugoslavia in 1941, Tito went
to work organising the Resistance, and Tito's Partisans became
legendary for their bravery and resourcefulness. In 1945, Tito
became president of the reconstituted Yugoslavia and ruled until
his death in 1980. Staro Selo first attracted visitors in 1952, when
his childhood home was opened as a memorial museum. Pilgrims
from all six republics and two autonomous provinces of the former
Yugoslavia visited the shrine of their beloved leader, as did ardent
socialists from all over the world, and still pay their respects today
on the anniversaries of his death and birthday.

PLITVICE LAKES NATIONAL PARK

A chance to explore the lakes, waterfalls and forests of Plitvice Lakes National Park. Lying just off the main road from Zagreb to Split, Plitvice can be visited as a day trip from the capital, or en route between the two cities. There are three hotels within the park, making an overnight stay possible.

War and Plitvice

The Plitvice region had a Serb majority until the War of Independence, and thus fell into the area that Croatian Serbs declared the Republic of Serbian Krajina. When hostilities began brewing in early 1991, Croatian police hastily set up a station in the park, and the first armed combat took place. Close to Entrance 2, you can see a steel-and-marble column dedicated to a police officer, Josip Jović, who at Easter in the same year became the first Croat to die in the war.

DISTANCE 10km (6¼ miles), including shuttle and boat trip
TIME A half day
START Entrance 2
END Entrance 1
POINTS TO NOTE

Plitvice is at its most beautiful in spring, when snowmelt increases the water volume, and in autumn. In winter local roads are occasionally blocked with snow, the lakes and falls may freeze, and, although the park is stunning, few of its facilities are operating.

To reach the park from Zagreb (167km/104 miles; about two hours), take the motorway A1 to the Cvor Bjelolasica exit and take Route 42 south. Alternatively, there are around 13 buses a day between Zagreb bus station (www.akz.hr) and the coast that stop at both park entrances on request; be sure the driver knows in advance where you want to get off.

The route described is just one possible way to approach the park. Walks of different lengths are signposted from both entrances. If you wish to see the dramatic Veliki slap first, start from Entrance 1.

Croatia's oldest and largest national park, **Plitvice Lakes** (Plitvička jezera; www.np-plitvicka-jezera.hr; daily 7am–8pm; charge) is the country's most visited inland destination, attracting up to 9,000 visitors a day in summer. Due to its outstanding natural beauty, it was proclaimed a Unesco World Heritage Site in 1979. Plitvice is a lovely place for walking, with a network of trails skirting the shores of the lakes and wooden footpaths criss-crossing the cascades.

A Unique Landscape

The park encompasses a succession of 16 lakes *(jezera)* linked by a series of spectacular waterfalls *(slapovi)*. These were formed by a geological process that has been going on for thousands of years and is still taking place today. When water flows over limestone, it picks up and then deposits calcium carbonate that encrusts algae and moss to form natural travertine barriers and dams. These, in turn, create lakes and cascades.

THE UPPER LAKES

There are two entrances to Plitvice: start your tour from **Entrance 2** ❶, close to the upper end of the system

of lakes and cascades, to follow the course of the water downriver to Entrance 1. If you are arriving from Zagreb, pass Entrance 1 and proceed to Entrance 2 at **Velika Poljana**, where you will find a large car park on the left-hand side of the road, plus a cluster of wooden chalets that house an information centre, a general store, an office dealing in private accommodation and a café.

From the car park, a wooden footbridge rises above the main road, bringing you to a footpath on the other side, which leads through the trees to **Hotel Jezero** *(see p.109)*. Behind the hotel, the path takes you past **Buffet Flora**, where you might stop for a drink, to a wooden hut selling entrance tickets.

From here, national park shuttle buses (price included in entrance fee) make regular runs to various locations in the park. Take a bus to **Station 4** at **Labudovac**, close to the first and highest lake, **Prošćansko** (639m/ 2,096ft above sea level).

Down to Goat's Lake

At Labudovac, turn right and follow the path downhill. The first lake that you will see on your left is **Okrugljak** ❷, site of a large cave topped with travertine 'curtains'. The next big lake down is **Galovac**, where the travertine has created a series of falls of exceptional beauty. Cross over the lake at the bottom and continue on the path alongside a succession of lakes downstream to **Kozjak Falls** ❸, which run into the largest lake, **Kozjak** (Kozjak

jezero means Goat's Lake). According to local legend, Kozjak earned its name after a herd of goats (*koza* means goat in Croatian) drowned here when crossing thin ice while

Above from far left: wooden footpath; rainbow formed in the spray of a waterfall; autumnal scene in the Upper Lakes.

Nikola Tesla

As you contemplate the thundering cascades of Veliki slap, note that the world-renowned physicist Nikola Tesla (1856–1943) came from the nearby village of Smiljan, close to Gospić, and undoubtedly visited Plitviče as a child. The son of a Serbian Orthodox priest, he later migrated to the US where he invented the electromagnetic motor and produced the first power system at the Niagara Falls. The unit for magnetic induction, Tesla (T), is named after him.

Below: Veliki slap.

trying to escape from wolves one winter. Most of the Plitvice lakes are named after people or things that have disappeared in them: Ciginovac was apparently named after a gypsy *(cigan)* who drowned in it while fishing, while Gavanovac was named after a rich man *(gavan)* who lost a hoard of treasure there.

Close to Kozjak Falls lies a **Landing Station**. Hop aboard the national park electric **ferry** (summer every 10 minutes, winter every 30 minutes; price included in entrance fee) for a 20-minute ride across the lake, passing by **Stefanie's Island** (Štefanijin otok). This is named after Princess Stefanie of Belgium, who married into the Habsburg family in the late 19th century – when Croatia was under Habsburg rule – and visited Plitvice in 1888.

THE LOWER LAKES

The boat journey ends at the north end of the lake, at **Kozjačka Draga** ❹, where you will find a leafy glade with a snack bar, picnic area and wooden kiosks selling local produce throughout the summer. From here, turn right to follow the water, which has by now taken on a brilliant emerald colour (due to the high mineral content of the limestone bedrock and the light) through the **Korana Canyon**.

Veliki Slap

Take the wooden walkway over **Milanovac Falls** ❺ and follow the path alongside the eastern side of the small lakes of **Milanovac** and **Gavanovac**. Cross over **Velike kascade** ❻ (Big Cascades) to walk alongside **Kaludjerovac**, then turn left to **Veliki**

slap 7 (Big Falls). Veliki slap, the park's highest and most dramatic waterfall (78m/256ft), is supplied by water from a separate source, the River Plitvica. Before the break-up of Yugoslavia, wedding ceremonies used to be held below the falls, and there are moves to restart this practice.

From here, all the waters meet to flow into the last and lowest lake, **Novakovica Brod** (503m/1,650ft above sea level), and form the River Korana, which flows through a steep-sided rocky canyon to Karlovac, where it meets the River Kupa, then proceeds to join first the River Sava then the Danube and flows east through Romania eventually to empty into the Black Sea.

Leave Veliki slap taking the wooden walkway that crosses the water just above **Sastavci Falls** (Sastavci slap),

then follow the steep and serpentine footpath uphill to **Entrance 1** at the northern end of the park. Here you will find a small general store selling basic foodstuffs and national park souvenirs, as well as **Lička kuča** restaurant, see ⑪①.

Alternatively, from Entrance 1, you can walk via a signposted path, or take a national park shuttle bus, back to Entrance 2 where you began.

Above from far left: path through the Lower Lakes; ripples; an electric ferry crosses Kozlak.

Below: life aquatic.

Food and Drink 🍴
① LIČKA KUČA
Entrance 1; Rastovača bb; tel: 053-751 023; €€
Plitvice is in the Lika region, which is known for its hearty, rustic fare. Although touristy, this restaurant remains an excellent place to sample local favourites such as *lička juha* (a heavy soup consisting of lamb, vegetables, lemon and sour cream) and *pladanj lička* (a mixed platter of meat and potatoes prepared under a *peka, see p.14*). If you do not eat meat, opt for trout, *škripevac* cheese and salad. As you wait for your meal, try a glass of potent *šlivovica* (plum brandy). The mock rustic interior and large open fire create a comfortable ambience.

Life in Plitvice
The park is densely forested with beech, as well as fir on land lying above 700m (2,300ft). The trees are vital to the ecosystem: without their roots the ground soil would be washed away. Also here are laurel, elderberry, holly, honeysuckle and ferns, plus orchids, lilies, hyacinths, cyclamen and peonies – many protected by law.

Swimming, fishing and hunting are prohibited, but if you are lucky you may spot one of the wild animals that live here, including deer, otters, badgers, lynx and wild boar, plus around 50 brown bears (the symbol of Plitvice). Packs of wolves also roam the area in winter. Birdwatchers should look out for woodpeckers and black storks; plus rare golden eagles and peregrine falcons in the woods; and grey herons, white-throated dippers and black-throated divers close to the water. For their part, the lakes support trout and chub, plus countless ducks and water snakes.

ISTRIAN COAST

Spend a day exploring the rugged Istrian coast. After a look at the Roman ruins of Pula, enjoy a seafood lunch at the Lim Channel, then proceed to the Byzantine mosaics of St Euphrasius' Basilica in Poreč, and end the day with sunset cocktails and dinner in Rovinj.

DISTANCE 130km (81 miles)
TIME A full day
START/END Pula
POINTS TO NOTE
To get the most out of this trip you need a car, although it is possible to follow the route from Pula to Poreč and on to Rovinj by bus. Local tourist offices *(see p.104)* should be able to advise on bus schedules. Make an early start, and bring comfortable shoes and a swimming costume.

Istria (Istra) takes its name from the first settlers here, the Illyrian tribe of the Histri. When the Romans conquered the peninsula in the 2nd century BC, they built fortified military towns on the former Histri settlements. The most important of these were Parentium (Poreč) and Pola (Pula).

Istria has always had close ties with Italy and from 1918 to 1945, following the collapse of the Habsburg Empire, it was subject to Italian sovereignty. Then, at the end of World War II, the territory was incorporated into Yugoslavia, although the Italian population was still recognised as a minority group, with its own schools and media, funded in part by the Italian government. Many Istrian towns and villages still have both Croatian and Italian names.

The rugged Istrian coastline is not so blessed with beaches as southern Croatia, but the cultural attractions here more than make up for it. Plus, there's a particularly agreeable 'Istrian' way of life that includes taking great pride in their local heritage, a devotion to good cuisine and a welcoming live and let live attitude. For a tour of inland Istria, see tour 6 *(p.48)*.

Food and Drink 🍴
① ULIKS
Trg Portorata I, Pula; tel: 052-219 158; daily 9am–9pm; €
A sculpture of James Joyce reminds you that this café was one of his favourite haunts. It remains immensely popular with locals and visitors, mostly because of its superb location.

Right: James Joyce.

PULA

On the southern tip of the Istrian peninsula lies **Pula ❶**, still the region's largest and most important city, just as it was 2,000 years ago when the Romans chose it as their administrative base. In addition to tourism, shipbuilding at Pula's Uljanik shipyard remains central to the local economy.

Roman Relics

In the centre of town you will find the monumental 1st-century AD Roman amphitheatre, known as the **Arena** (daily May–Sept 8am–9pm, Oct–Apr 8.30am–4.30pm; charge). This three-storey oval structure was designed to seat 23,000 spectators and is the sixth-largest surviving building of its kind in the world. During the 16th century, the Venetians carried off a good number of Istria's Roman relics, and it seems that they even considered dismantling the arena and rebuilding it in Venice. Today the ancient amphitheatre – whose exterior is still remarkably intact – plays host to a lively programme of summer festivals and rock concerts (see p.19).

Cross Flavijevska and the small park to arrive at **Riva**, the seafront promenade. Turn left, passing the harbour and yacht marina, to arrive at the **Cathedral** (Katedrala; summer daily 7am–noon and 4–6pm, winter Mass only; free), which started as a 5th-century basilica, built on the foundations of a Roman temple. Its 17th-century bell tower was built of stone taken from the arena.

On the other side of the cathedral, follow Kandlerova to arrive at the **Forum**, today Pula's main square and once, as the name indicates, the Roman forum. Note the well-preserved **Temple of Augustus** that stands next to the 13th-century Town Hall (Gradska vijećnica). From the Forum, take traffic-free **Sergijevaca** on the southeast corner to arrive at the imposing **Sergius Arch** (also known as Zlatna vrata – Golden Gate), which was erected in 27BC.

Close by stands the house in which Irish writer James Joyce lived for a brief period in 1904–5 when he worked as an English teacher at the Berlitz School. In the same building is the pleasant café **Uliks** (Ulysses), see ⑪①.

Above from far left: Rovinj; Pula's Arena; Sergius Arch.

Vodnjan's Mummies

In the heart of this sleepy and unremarkable Istrian town lies a truly macabre attraction. Behind the altar of the stately late 18th-century Church of St Blaise (Crkva sv. Baža; summer daily 7am–noon and 4–6pm, winter Mass only; free) lie the desiccated remains of six saints. The clothed, intact bodies of St Leon Bembo, St John Olini and St Nicolosa Bursa are behind glass, as well as body parts of three other saints. For unknown reasons, the bodies and body parts have failed to decompose, although the skin and nails have darkened and dried, making the corpses look curiously wooden. The church reliquary contains several hundred more relics enclosed in glass receptacles, including the undecayed tongue of St Mary of Egypt.

Lim Channel

The Lim Channel's name comes from the Latin word *limes* (border), as the long and narrow channel once divided two Roman provinces. It was formed when the coastline sank during the last Ice Age and water flooded the Draga valley. The karst cliffs also harbour several caves, of which the best-known is Romuald's Cave, named after a Benedictine monk who once camped out there. You can book a boat tour from Rovinj or Poreč, which includes a channel tour and a visit to the cave. The Rovinj or Poreč tourist offices (www.tzgrovinj.hr; www.istra.com/porec) will have more details.

Below: Madonna and Child at the Basilica of St Euphrasius.

LIM CHANNEL

From Pula heading north, take Route 3 passing **Vodnjan** ❷ *(see margin, p.43)* and Bale (22km/13½ miles). En route you will see several *kašuni*, small circular stone structures peculiar to Istria, built by local farmers. A few kilometres after Brajkoviči a sign saying 'Limski kanal' will direct you to the left. Follow the road downhill to the parking lot for the **Lim Channel** ❸ (Limski kanal; also known as Lim Fjord or Limska Draga Fjord). Lined by steep forested walls, the 10km (6-mile) long fjord is one of Istria's most dramatic sights. The clean, pure water has made the fjord a prime spot for farmed mussels and oysters; two of Istria's best seafood restaurants are located here. This is a good place to stop for a swim and a seafood lunch at either **Viking**, see ⑪②, or **Fjord**.

POREČ

After lunch, return to the main road and head north. Head past Lovreč to Baderna and then take Route 302 west to **Poreč** ❹ (about 25km/16 miles). The historic town centre is a fascinating place to wander, and still bears traces of Poreč's many occupiers, from the Romans to the Byzantines and the Venetians. A network of seaside resorts stretches north and south of town, making Poreč a busy place at the height of summer.

Leave your car in the large waterfront car park and take the coastal promenade, Nikole Tesle, into the Old Town. You will quickly arrive at Trg Slobode, a large square lined with cafés.

City Museum

The cobbled street that veers off to your right is **Decumanus**, which forms a central axis the length of the Old Town. The straight streets follow the original Roman plan, while the elegant building façades are clearly Venetian-inspired. Follow Decumanus a few blocks and on the left at no. 9 you will see the Baroque Sinčić Palace, which is home to the **City Museum** (Gradski muzej; tel: 052-431 085; summer 10am–1pm and 6–9pm, winter 10am–noon; charge). It contains prehistoric pottery, fragments of Roman sculpture and portraits of local notables.

Basilica of St Euphrasius

Continue south on Decumanus a short way until you see a sign to the right, 'Bazilika', which brings you directly into the 6th-century atrium of the **Basilica of St Euphrasius** (Eufrazijeva bazilika; daily 7am–7pm; free). What started as a little oratory in the 4th century grew to become a basilica in the 5th century. In the 6th century

Bishop Euphrasius expanded it into a complex that included an episcopal palace, an atrium, a baptistery and a chapel. Adopting the lavish style of Byzantium's 'Golden Age', all the buildings were ornamented with mosaics. Much of the original architecture and nearly all the mosaics remain intact.

The silence and simplicity of the interior – rough tiled floor, bare walls and sturdy columns with discreet ornamentation – produce a reverential atmosphere in this Unesco-protected treasure. Be sure to look at the splendid golden mosaics in the apse, which were created by craftsmen from Constantinople and Ravenna.

On the opposite side of the atrium stands the baptistery, presided over by a 16th-century **bell tower**. Climb to the top for magnificent views; on a fine day you might even see Venice.

Go back to Decumanus and continue to **Trg M. Gupca**, a square with a raised garden and benches where locals gather to exchange news in the shade of the trees. Keep on the main axis and to the left you will see the 13th-century **Romanesque House** (Romanička kuća) with a well-preserved wooden balcony.

Temples and Monuments
On the tip of the peninsula lies **Trg Marafor**, the forum in Roman times, and site of two ancient temples. In the park at the end of the square stand fragments of the **Temple of Neptune**, built in the 2nd century AD to honour the god of the sea. Too

little remains of the other temple to identify it.

Along the southern side of the peninsula runs **Obala maršala Tita**. The town's oldest hotels look out over the harbour from here, and there are numerous boats to and from the island of **Sveti Nikola** (a one-hour return trip), which is the area's best place for bathing. You can also see two well-kept monuments bearing the Red Star to commemorate those Croats and Italians who opposed Fascism during World War II; a rare sight in Croatia today.

Stop off at **Barilla Pizzeria**, see ⑪③, if you are feeling hungry, then leave Poreč by car, taking the coastal road south past the tourist complexes of Plava Laguna and Zelena Laguna. Drive through Funtana – named after the freshwater springs the Romans used to supply their summer villas – and then turn left before the town of **Vrsar**, home of **Koversada**, the renowned naturist camp *(see margin, p.20)*. The road now turns inland and passes through the villages of Flengi and Kloštar.

Food and Drink

② VIKING
Lim Channel; tel: 052-448 223; daily 11am–11pm; €€
Sample Lim seafood at Viking, which is situated right on the waterfront with a large terrace. Try the oysters on ice, noodles with scampi and porcini mushrooms, or baked fish with potatoes.

③ BARILLA PIZZERIA
Eufrazijeva 2, Poreč; tel: 052-452 742; daily 11am–midnight; €–€€
This traditional Italian-style pizzeria serves up tasty pasta and pizza dishes on a lively terrace overlooking one of Poreč's most beautiful squares.

Rovinj Aquarium

If you are interested in underwater life, stop at the Rovinj Aquarium (Obala G. Paliage 5; tel: 052-804 700; June–Sept: daily 9am–9pm, Apr–May and Oct: Sat–Sun 10am–6pm; charge), about 100m/yds beyond the parking lot and signposted on the right. The fish in the aquarium are indigenous to the Adriatic.

Below: fishermen preparing their nets.

ROVINJ

At the village of Brajkoviči, turn right, passing through Rovinjsko Selo, to arrive in **Rovinj** ❺. The town, founded on an island, was fortified during the Middle Ages. In the 18th century the narrow channel separating it from the mainland was filled, and urban development extended beyond the walls. Thus the Old Town, confined to a small peninsula presided over by a hilltop cathedral, remains unspoilt: indeed, it is possibly Istria's most attractive port town. The many centuries that Rovinj spent under Venetian rule are evident in the Venetian-Gothic windows and the St Mark lion motif that crops up throughout the town.

Park along the waterfront and then follow Obala palih boraca to the town centre. You will soon arrive at **Trg maršala Tita**. Amid the tourist hubbub, there is still one decent café: **Viecia Batana**, see ⑪④, at no. 8, is an atmospheric place to stop for a rest.

Rovinj Museum

At the northern end of the square is the **Rovinj Museum** (Zavičajni musej Rovinj; tel 052-816 720; www.muzej-rovinj.com; summer Tue–Fri 9am–3pm and 7–10pm, Sat–Sun 9am–2pm and 7–10pm, winter Tue–Sat 9am–3pm; charge), with halls devoted to Old Masters such as the Renaissance artists Giovanni Bellini and Bonifazio de Pitati and Baroque artists Marco Ricci, Antonio Zanchi, Girolamo Romanino and Nicola Grassi. Local and contemporary Croatian artists are also represented, and there is an archaeological collection.

Cathedral of St Euphemia

A few steps further north, pass through the 17th-century Baroque **Balbi Arch** (Balbijev luk). From here take any of the narrow cobbled streets that climb towards the hilltop **Cathedral of St Euphemia** (Katedrala sv. Eufenija; summer 10am–6pm, winter variable hours; free). Modelled after the St Mark's bell tower in Venice, the 60m (197ft) high Baroque tower is perhaps Rovinj's most defining feature. The remains of St Euphemia, who was martyred during the reign of Emperor

Diocletian (245–312AD), are said to lie in a sarcophagus inside the cathedral. According to legend, the casket floated out to sea from Constantinople, and was washed ashore here in 800AD.

Seafront Sunset

Return to town by taking the stepped street of **Grisia**, which becomes an open-air art gallery every year on the second Sunday in August. From Trg maršala Tita turn right onto Obala Pina Budicina and stroll along the quay with the rest of the early evening crowd. You will shortly come to **Sv. Križa**, an excellent vantage point to watch the sunset. The best place to view the show is from **Monte Carlo Caffe-Bar**, see ⑪⑤. For dinner you could stop at the nearby **Konoba Veli Jože**, see ⑪⑥, to sample Istrian specialities.

To return to Pula (32km/20 miles), head south, passing through the small settlement of Spanidiga, following signs to Bale. Once you reach Bale, turn right towards Vodnjan and then on to Pula.

Left: boat trip to Red Island.

Food and Drink 🍴

④ VIECIA BATANA
Trg maršala Tita 8; daily 8am–10pm; €
Especially popular with locals for morning coffee, this café overlooks the harbour and offers a perfect vantage point to observe the comings and goings of boats, especially during annual regattas. Good cakes and ice cream served too.

⑤ MONTE CARLO CAFFE-BAR
Sv. Križa 21; tel: 052-830 683; daily noon–midnight; €
Just sit on the rocks, drink in hand, and gaze at the sea as it changes colours while the sun sets.

⑥ KONOBA VELI JOŽE
Sv. Križa 1; tel: 052-876 337; daily 11am–1am; €€
Here you can taste old-fashioned Istrian fare such as *fuži* (pasta) with goulash and *bakalar na bijelo* (salt-cod pâté).

Active Rovinj

Within easy reach of Rovinj's hilly Old Town is a wealth of opportunities for active travellers. Just a short boat ride away (every half-hour from the boat dock in front of Trg maršala Tita) is Crveni otok (Red Island), a summer favourite for its numerous swimming coves, some of which are reserved for naturists. The crystal waters off Rovinj are a magnet for scuba-divers, especially those wishing to explore the wreck of the *Baron Gautsch*, an Austrian ocean liner sunk in 1914 (you can arrange a dive through Nadi Scuba, J. Dobrile 11; tel 052-813 290; www.scuba.hr).

Back on land is Zlatni Rt-Punta Corrente, a magnificent protected forest on the southern side of Rovinj. Cypresses, Douglas firs, cedars and stone pines offer shade for a refreshing stroll along the landscaped promenades. Too sedate? Go vertical. A Venetian quarry on the park's seaside has dozens of rock-climbing routes, suitable for all levels. Also near Rovinj, 8km (5 miles) to the southwest, is the Palud swamp (June–Aug daily 9am–9pm; charge), an ornithological reserve harbouring over 200 bird species.

HEART OF ISTRIA

Overlooked by many tourists, the rolling countryside of inland Istria offers such treasures as the dramatic abyss at Pazin, remarkable frescoes at Beram and the stunning hill towns of Motovun and Grožnjan. You can also stop off at Hum, self-proclaimed 'world's smallest town'.

Below: rustic items in the Ethnographic Museum.

DISTANCE 100km (62 miles)

TIME One or two days

START/END Pazin

POINTS TO NOTE

This itinerary is designed as a round trip from Pazin and requires a car, which can easily be hired in tourist centres on the coast if that is where you are based. If you are restricted to public transport, you can still cover part of the route: take a local bus from Pazin to Motovun and a local bus or train from Pazin to Buzet. If you wish to spend two days doing this tour, consider staying overnight in Pazin (see p.110).

Numerous visitors to Istria (Istra) head straight for the coast, but the region most cherished by the majority of Croatians is **Srce Istre** (Heart of Istria). This inland terrain of hills and valleys, planted with woods and vineyards, is best-known for the romantic silhouettes of its hill towns. While Pazin and eastern Istria were, for several hundred years, ruled by Austria, the area west of Pazin was answerable to Venice. The two regions were only united in 1805, as one of Napoleon's many geographical revisions.

PAZIN

The tour begins at **Pazin ❶**, inland Istria's largest town, which for centuries was known by its German name, Mitterburg (Central Town). The name is fitting for a town right in the centre of Istria that is neither large nor small, neither ancient nor modern, neither prosperous nor poor. Pazin is a pleasant and easygoing town unused to seeing much tourism, which in itself makes it worth a visit. It does mean, however, that if you stay in Pazin, you should be aware that there are no notable restaurants in town. Just 7km (5 miles) southeast out of town, however, is the homespun food of **Marino**, see ⑪①.

Pazin Abyss

The settlement developed around a castle built above a dramatic gorge, the **Pazin Abyss** (Pazinska Jama). The 100m (330ft) deep chasm is a natural phenomenon formed by the River Pazinčića, which flows into a semicircular cave called, appropriately enough, Dante's lobby. A series of lakes and subterranean canals siphons the flow into a network of streams and tributaries that underlie the porous rock. One large underground lake lies directly under the castle, but the thickly forested terrain blocks a view of the entrance.

The seemingly bottomless pit set the French author Jules Verne wondering if it leads to the Lim Channel *(see p.44)*. It most likely does not, but that did not stop Verne from writing *Mathias Sandorf* (1885), where the novel's hero jumps into the Pazin Abyss and emerges in the Lim Channel.

Pazin Castle

A stroll around the well-maintained **castle** perched on a cliff over the abyss makes it easy to imagine such improbable adventures. The castle houses the **Ethnographic Museum of Istria** (Etnografski muzej Istre; tel: 052-645 040; winter Tue–Thur 10am–3pm, Fri noon–5pm, Sat–Sun 11am–5pm, summer Tue–Sun 10am–6pm; charge), with well-displayed collections of traditional costumes, farm implements and the like. Also here is the **Civic Museum of Pazin** (Gradski muzej). During the summer, concerts are held in the courtyard, and there is a week of festivities in mid-June celebrating Jules Verne.

BERAM

From Pazin take the main road west for Poreč. After 5km (3 miles), take the narrow road to the right leading up a hill to **Beram ❷**. This site was first settled by the Illyrians as a prehistoric hillfort *(gradina)* and later became a fortified medieval town. Now a sleepy village, Beram wakes up once a year, when local farmers bring freshly fermented wine here to be blessed on **St Martin's Day** *(see margin, right)*.

> ## Food and Drink 🍴
> ① **MARINO**
> Gračišće 75, Pazin; tel: 052-687 081; Mon–Tue and Thur–Sat 2–11pm, Sun 10am–11pm; €€
> At the entrance to nearly abandoned Gračišće is this restaurant-tavern. Vegetarians will have a tough time, but there's nothing industrial about the homemade sausages and home-smoked ham. The rustic decor stimulates a hearty appetite.

Above from far left: Istrian vineyards; grape harvest; Pazin Castle and Abyss.

St Martin's Day On 11 November Beram (along with Zagorje, *see pp.34–7*) celebrates Martinje (St Martin's Day). A 'bishop' blesses the must (fermenting grape juice), warning that it is a sin to make *delanec* (wine fortified with added sugar, diluted with water or abused in any other way). After this ritual, the townsfolk tuck into a feast of roast goose and *mlinci* (baked noodles) plus, of course, an endless flow of local wine.

Below: *Danse Macabre* in Beram's Church of St Mary.

The tiny church of St Mary is locked in order to protect the treasured frescoes. To get the key, proceed to the town centre, where the phone number of the church custodian is posted on the noticeboard at the town entrance. At the time of writing, the number was 052-622 903. The custodian lives right nearby and is usually able to meet you within a few minutes in the town square with the key. Together you will drive the kilometre or so to the church.

Beram's Frescoes

The main reason to visit Beram, however, is to see the extraordinary 15th-century frescoes in the **Church of St Mary** (Crkva sv. Marija na Škriljinah; *see margin, left*). The interior walls are entirely covered with a vivid and colourful cycle of frescoes that date from 1474. Over time they were hidden by mortar and whitewashed, only to be rediscovered and restored in 1913. Painted by local artist Vincent of Kastav and his assistants, these frescoes were not only decorative, but also served as a 'Bible for the Illiterate'. The biblical scenes depicted were intended to educate and amuse the congregation. The frescoes feature a backdrop of 15th-century Istrian countryside, thereby giving us a fascinating record of life in those times. The most notable piece is the allegorical *Danse Macabre* above the main door. Detailed explanations in English are available.

MOTOVUN

From Beram proceed north 16km (10 miles) to **Motovun** ❸. As you navigate the treacherous hairpin bends, you may find it of interest to know that the

eminent American racing driver Mario Andretti (winner of the Indianapolis Race in 1969 and Formula 1 world champion in 1978) was born in these parts in 1940. The town is also known for its annual five-day **Motovun Film Festival** (late July–early Aug; www.motovunfilmfestival.com).

The car park is about 100m/yds before the entrance to the town (in high season there is a charge for parking). Take the cobbled street uphill to arrive at the first town gate, built at the beginning of the 14th century and adorned by reliefs of Venetian lions. Further uphill, the second gate leads to Motovun's main square, which is dominated by the 17th-century **Church of St Stephen** (Crkva sv. Stjepan). Built according to plans by one of the founding fathers of Renaissance architecture, Andrea Palladio, this Renaissance-Baroque jewel harbours several treasures. Note the 17th-century painting of *The Last Supper* behind the main altar and the 18th-century ceiling paintings. Next to the church is the 13th-century Gothic **bell tower** that looms over the town.

Across from the church is the Renaissance **Municipal Palace** and annexes (closed to the public), built between the 14th and 19th centuries. The medieval **well** in front of the church dates from the 14th century, when the town drew water from the cistern underneath the town square.

Town Walls

Just outside the second gate is the **Hotel Kaštel**, see ⑪②, with a large

---

Food and Drink 🍴

② HOTEL KAŠTEL

Trg Andrea Antico 7, Motovun; 052-681 687; daily 8am–midnight; €

Shaded by trees, the terrace here has the best location in town. The restaurant, which serves dishes like pasta with truffles and beef stew, is good but pricey; drinks are more reasonable.

DIOCLETIAN'S PALACE

Begin the day with a coffee at any of the many cafés that line the seafront promenade (Riva or Obala hrvatskog narodnog Preporoda). The southern façade of **Diocletian's Palace** (Dioklecijanova palaca) provides a perfect suntrap, and the café terraces here remain open almost all the year round.

The palace combined the qualities of a villa with those of a fortified military camp. Four sturdy outer walls each have a monumental gate that provides controlled access to the complex. The palace resembles a walled medieval town with streets and passages surrounding a central square that is dominated by the cathedral. The southern façade, now giving onto the Riva, originally rose directly from the water, and boats could enter the complex from the sea.

Podrum

Walk along the Riva and find an opening between nos 22 and 23 to enter the dark underground halls known as the **podrum ❶**. This vast space served as a substructure to the palace above, and was probably used for storage. One passage through the halls leads to the peristyle above and is lined with stalls that sell pictures, ceramics, jewellery and handmade souvenirs. The rest of the halls can be visited (daily 9am–6pm; charge), but the vast echoing chambers are eerily empty.

Above from far left:
Split's harbour; the vestibule's domed roof in Diocletian's Palace; strolling the Riva.

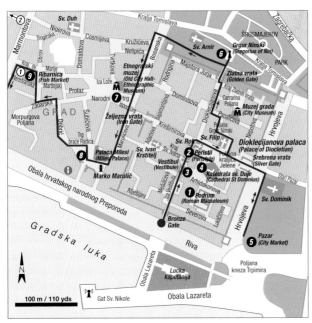

Beaches

While not commonly considered a beach resort, Split does have places to take a refreshing swim. The closest to town is Bačvice, a sandy but crowded beach, just a short walk southeast. A little further out is Kašjuni cove, past the Meštrović Gallery on Šetalište Ivana Meštrovića.

Below: touching the toe of Grgur Ninski.

Peristyle

From the podrum ascend a steep flight of stone steps and you will arrive on the **peristyle ❷** (peristil). In Diocletian's time this colonnaded square was the principal public space within the walls. Today, it remains a popular meeting point, and from late afternoon into the early hours of the morning, groups of students congregate here. During the summer festival *(see p.19)*, the peristyle's dramatic quality sets the scene for a series of outdoor opera performances and concerts.

Vestibule

Directly above the podrum exit stands the **vestibule ❸**, the grand entrance into Diocletian's seafront quarters. The domed roof would originally have been decorated with mosaics, and the walls faced with marble. Groups singing *klapa*, traditional Dalmatian plainsong *(see p.18)*, are known to travel all the way from the islands to take advantage of the vestibule's exceptional acoustics.

Cathedral of St Dominius

After Diocletian's death in 316AD, his body was enclosed in a sarcophagus and placed in the centre of an octagonal mausoleum. Situated on the eastern side of the peristyle, the emperor's resting place is now the **Cathedral of St Domnius ❹** (Katedrala sv. Duje; July–Aug daily 8am–noon and 4–7pm, Sept–June daily 10am–noon; charge), which is ironic because Diocletian despised Christianity with a passion and instigated the last great period of martyrdom and suffering for Christians. Thousands of believers were tortured to death. The fact that both his wife and daughter were Christians is something of an anomaly. Later inhabitants of the palace converted Diocletian's mausoleum into an early Christian church dedicated to St Domnius, after Bishop Domnius of Salona, who was one of the many victims of the late emperor's purges.

As you enter the cathedral, note the original wooden doors, which date back to 1214. Carved by Andrija Buvina, a local sculptor, they depict 28 scenes from the *Life of Christ*. To the right of

the cathedral bell tower sits a proud Egyptian sphinx, made of black granite and dating from 1500BC.

You can climb the magnificent 13th-century Romanesque **bell tower**. From the top, some 60m (200ft) above the town, you can get a better perspective of the urban layout.

Grgur was a 9th-century bishop who challenged Rome by advocating that the Croatian Church use the Slav tongue and Glagolitic script, as opposed to Latin. Tradition has it that if you touch the statue's toe and make a wish it will be granted. The toe has been worn golden by the hands of hopeful passers-by.

Above from far left: cathedral bell tower; Egyptian sphinx; the cathedral's wooden doors date back to the early 13th century.

CITY MARKET

From the peristyle, turn right onto Poljana kraljice Jelene to head for the city market. Leave the palace through the **Silver Gate** (Srebrena vrata), which was discovered and restored in the 1950s, having been concealed behind brick walls for centuries. The **City Market** ❺ (Pazar; Mon–Sat 6am–1pm, Sun 6–11am) offers a chaotic array of seasonal fruit and vegetables, homemade cheeses and salamis, honey and herbal teas. If you are planning a picnic, this is where to pick up supplies.

Afterwards, retrace your steps through the Silver Gate and take the second turning on the right to pass through Poljana Grgur Ninski. Now turn left on Papalićeva, then right on Dioklecijanova, to reach **Golden Gate** (Zlatna vrata), which was originally the main entrance into the palace.

GRGUR NINSKI

Just outside the gate stands an imposing statue of **Grgur Ninski** ❻. This monument was created by Ivan Meštrović *(see p.58)* in 1929, and originally placed on the peristyle to commemorate the 1,000th anniversary of the Split synod.

NARODNI TRG

From the statue, follow the path right (west) through the garden that runs parallel with the outer walls, then turn left into Bosanska. You are now within the second area of town development. Follow Bosanska to arrive on **Narodni trg** ❼, the main town square.

In the 11th century Split enjoyed a period of material wealth and urban expansion. Medieval town houses were constructed alongside the wide thoroughfares of the ancient palace, resulting in a dark labyrinth of narrow walkways. Split also extended westward, and the **Iron Gate** (Željezna vrata) became the internal link between the old and new parts of town. When this newer zone was fortified in the 14th century, Narodni trg took over the role of municipal centre, while the peristyle remained the focus of religious activity.

Below: produce from the City Market.

Ethnographic Museum
The Venetians added a town hall on the square, identifiable by the Venetian-Gothic triple arches on the ground floor, which is now the **Ethnographic Museum** (Etnografski muzej; tel: 021-343 108; Sat 9am–1pm, also Sept–June Mon–Fri 9am–2pm, and Sept and June

Above from far left: garfish at the Fish Market; Veli Varoš; sculpture, Meštrović Gallery; the peaceful Marjan peninsula.

Local Hero
Ivan Meštrović was the finest artist to emerge from Croatia. Born in 1883 when Croatia was still part of the Austro-Hungarian Empire, Meštrović studied in Vienna and devoted much of his early work to the theme of Croatian independence. He later turned to religious themes, and was the first living artist to be honoured with an exhibition at the Metropolitan Museum of Art in New York. He became a US citizen in 1954 but bequeathed a substantial core of his work to Croatia.

Below: as Marmontova approaches the sea, loop right to find Trg Republike, an Austro-Hungarian imperial square with attractive colonnades.

5–8pm, July–Aug Mon–Fri 9am–9pm; charge), displaying a collection of Dalmatian folk costumes. The complex originally included the adjoining Rector's Palace and a theatre that was demolished in 1821 by the Habsburgs. For their part, the Austrians erected a Secessionist building at the far end of the square.

TRG BRAĆE RADIĆA

Leave Narodni trg by Maruličeva, a narrow street to your right as you face the Iron Gate and the 15th-century town clock. This will take you into **Trg braće Radića ❽**, a small square just one block back from the Riva, closed to the south by two octagonal 15th-century towers. At the square's centre stands a statue of **Marko Marulić** by Meštrović. The 15th century witnessed the birth of Croatian literature: Dalmatia was the centre of this movement, and Marulić's *Judita* is usually cited as the first play to be written in Croatian. Published in 1521, it recounts the biblical story of Judith and was written as a call to arms against the Ottoman occupation.

FISH MARKET

Walk the length of the square and take Dobrić, then turn left on Zadarska and immediately right on Obrov to arrive at the indoor **Fish Market ❾** (Ribarnica; Mon–Sat 6am–noon, Sun 6–10am) on Kraj sv. Marije. The peculiar smell here is not just the fish: next door stands another Secessionist building, which is the home of a private sulphur spa.

Lunch Options
Now is a good time to consider lunch. If the fish market has inspired you, stop for lunch at **Nostromo**, see ⑪①, beside the market. Or for pizza, turn right on Marmontova, then take the second left for Tončićeva, to arrive at **Galija**, see ⑪②, the best pizzeria in town. If you have shopped for a picnic, turn left on Marmontova, then right on the Riva, and stroll along the seafront to the gardens of the **Church of St Stephen ❿** (Crkva sv. Stjepan) on the promontory, where you can eat in the shade of pine trees overlooking the sea.

ARCHAEOLOGICAL MUSEUM

After lunch you could visit the **Museum of Croatian Archaeological Monuments ⓫** (Muzeja Hrvatskih arheoloških spomenika; Šetalište Ivana Meštrovića; tel: 021-358 455; Tue–Sat 9am–4pm, Sun 9am–noon; charge) near St Stephen when you turn left on on Šetalište Ivana Meštrovića. The museum traces the religious art of the first Croat settlers from the 7th–15th centuries. Some of the carvings on display feature interlaced geometric patterns reminiscent of Celtic art. The exhibits are labelled in Croatian, but you can buy an English-language guidebook at the entrance. Check out the outdoor terrace's group of *stećci*, monolithic tombstones dating back to the cult of the Bogomils (an anticlerical, anti-imperial sect that enjoyed widespread popularity in the Balkans between the 10th and 15th centuries).

MEŠTROVIĆ GALLERY

Afterwards, walk for 10 minutes further along the same road until you reach no. 46, the **Meštrović Gallery** ⑫ (Galerija Meštrović; tel: 021-340 800; summer Tue–Sun 9am–7pm, winter Tue–Sat 9am–4pm, Sun 10am–3pm; charge). Ivan Meštrović *(see margin, left)* designed the villa as both a home and an exhibition space. Inside you can see his early pieces, which were heavily influenced by the Secessionist movement in Vienna, where he studied, and also his later works, which portray tortured, screaming figures that reflect the anguish he and millions of others suffered during World War II.

The gallery entrance ticket is also valid for **Kaštelet** ⑬, at no. 39, where you can see another Meštrović masterpiece: a series of woodcarvings portraying the *Life of Christ*, housed within a small church.

MARJAN PENINSULA

Round off the afternoon with a walk back to town across **Marjan** peninsula. Catch bus no. 12 from opposite Kaštelet, and disembark at the gateway into **Bene Beach** ⑭, which fringes the western edge of Marjan. The peninsula is planted with dense pine woods, and several well-kept paths offer beautiful views and a welcome retreat from city life. On the highest point there flies a Croatian flag.

Keep to the path along the southern side for the finest views, and pass the 15th-century **Church of St Jerome** (Crkva sv. Jere) and a medieval cave **hermitage** built into the cliffs. The walk, which takes about 40 minutes, ends at the 13th-century Romanesque **Church of St Nicolas** (Crkva sv. Nikola). Close by, the **Vidilica**, see ⑪③, terrace bar, is ideal for an early-evening drink.

Veli Varoš

Return to town via the stone steps of Senjska, passing through the appealingly ramshackle quarter of **Veli Varoš** ⑮. Continue down to Trumbićeva obala to try the hearty fare of **Fife**, see ⑪④. From here continue east along the seafront to return to the town centre.

Checking the Flag

A renowned local journalist, the late Miljenko Smoje, said that every morning he would look up to Marjan and check the flag so he knew which country he was in. In the past century Split has been part of Austro-Hungary, and the Kingdom of Yugoslavia; it has been occupied by Italy and Germany; it was part of the Federal Republic of Yugoslavia, and is now an independent Croatia.

Food and Drink 🍴

① NOSTROMO
Kraj sv. Marije 10; tel: 091-405 6666; www.restoran-nostromo.hr; daily 6am–midnight; €€
There's no question about the freshness of the seafood here, as the restaurant is located right on the fish market. Oysters, mussels, shrimp and the daily catch are simply but expertly prepared in this nautically themed eatery.

② GALIJA
Tončićeva 12; tel: 021-389 288; daily 11am–11pm; €
The pizza here never fails to delight. A tasty crust and the freshest toppings are the elements that make Galija the most popular pizza place in town. Salads and pastas round out the menu.

③ VIDILICA
Nazorov prilaz 1; tel: 021-394 925
The setting here is stunning, with views of the sea, the islands, the harbour and city's terracotta rooftops. No meals, just cakes.

④ FIFE
Trumbićeva obala 11; tel: 021-345 223; €
This casual place serves up simple but scrumptious plates of fried and grilled meat and fish, black risotto, and *palačinke* (pancakes) washed down by local wine.

AROUND SPLIT

This tour takes you along the coast to the evocative Roman ruins of Salona, on to the Unesco World Heritage Site of Trogir, then down to experience the Biokovo Nature Park, returning to Split with a stop at Baška Voda.

DISTANCE 175km (109 miles)

TIME A full day

START/END Split

POINTS TO NOTE

A car is recommended for this tour, but it can be done by public transport if you allow two days. From May to October there are regular shuttle boats from Split harbour to Trogir. There also are numerous buses running down the coast, serving Trogir, Solin, Makarska and Baška Voda from the Split bus station (see www.ak-split.hr). To visit the Biokovo Nature Park by jeep, you should allot one day and leave Split early in the morning.

Brač

Just half an hour across the water from Split by ferry is Brač, Croatia's third-largest island and the location of Žlatni Rat (Golden Cape) near Bol. This shingle peninsula cuts scenically into the Adriatic, attracting countless sun-lovers and boat cruises during summer. Bol itself has a pleasant Old Town and is a centre for walks in the surrounding hills.

The suburbs of Split are unattractive and overdeveloped, but a few kilometres further on the sprawl gives way to an indented coastline backed by high mountains. The towns and villages here are rich in history and architecture, and provide a break from busy Split.

SALONA

Leave Split and head north, following signs to Trogir. After a few kilometres you will reach Solin. Little more than a suburb of Split, Solin would be unremarkable except for the extraordinary

Roman ruins of **Salona** ❶ on the suburb's outskirts. Park outside the main entrance, where there is a small **archaeological museum** (May–Oct Mon–Sat 7am–7pm, Sat 9am–7pm, Sun 9am–1pm, Nov–Apr Mon–Sat 9am–1pm; charge for entering museum and main archaeological site).

First on your left is **manastirine**, a vast necropolis where many of the Christian victims of Diocletian's persecution were buried. Follow the path bordered with cypresses south to Salona's **city wall**. South of the wall is a covered **aqueduct**, dating from the 1st century AD, and ahead of you are the remains of a 5th-century **cathedral** and **public baths**. The most impressive part of Salona is undoubtedly the **amphitheatre** at the western end, which could accommodate up to 18,000 spectators.

TROGIR

After Solin turn off from the D8 and follow the old Adriatic highway (Jadranska magistrala) until it rejoins the D8 road further along the coast. After 20km (12½ miles) you will arrive in **Trogir** ❷, a Renaissance jewel. Park in the large car park on the mainland just north of the Old Town, which is situated on a small island between the mainland and Čiovo island.

To reach the Old Town, cross a small bridge at the southern end of the car park. Once on the island pause for a moment to admire the town walls. Protected by these thick walls and with the sea on one side and hills on the other, an extraordinary cultural life developed in Trogir from the 13th to 15th centuries. The finely adorned buildings in Trogir's medieval core recall the height of Dalmatian artistry, even as cafés, restaurants and souvenir shops crowd around them.

Cathedral of St Lawrence

Pass through the 17th-century Baroque **Land Gate** (Kopnena vrata) crowned by a statue of the town's patron saint, St John of Trogir (Sv. Ivan Trogirski). Turn left after the entrance gate and then take the second street on the right to arrive on the main square, Trg Ivana Pavla II.

Here you will find Trogir's most impressive buildings, including the **Cathedral of St Lawrence** (Katedrala sv. Lovrijenca; summer 9am–8pm, winter 9am–noon and 4–7pm; charge). This monumental edifice was built between 1200 and 1598. The earliest and most beautiful element is the main portal, which, richly decorated in Romanesque style, features saints, Apostles, animals and grotesques. The door is guarded by nude Adam and Eve figures, both standing on lions. Attributed to Master Radovan, the most celebrated Croatian sculptor of the time, the piece dates from 1240.

The interior is equally impressive. Halfway along the left aisle stands the 15th-century Renaissance **St John's Chapel** by Dalmatian sculptor Nikola Firentinac. On display here is a Gothic sarcophagus decorated with a relief of

Above from far left:
Latin inscription on the Roman ruins at Salona; rowboat at Makarska; remains of Salona's amphitheatre.

History of Salona
Salona was first settled by the Illyrians in the 2nd century BC, and then conquered by the Romans in 78BC, who made it the capital of the province of Dalmatia. Salona flourished as a major metropolis until 614AD, when the Slavs and Avars swept in and demolished it, chasing Salona's inhabitants on to Split.

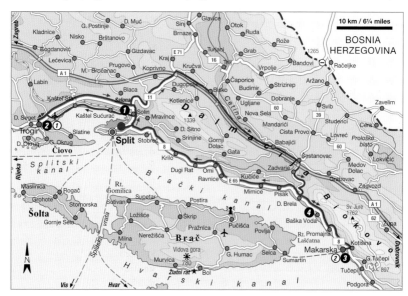

Shell Museum

The Franciscan Monastery in Makarska has a massive shell collection (over 3,000 amassed from around the world), but it's only open one hour a day (Mon–Sat 11am–noon charge). In order to see the museum, shell buffs may want to do this tour in reverse, starting in Makarska, taking the motorway to Trogir and the coastal road back to Split. The monastery is easy to find. Follow the seafront promenade to join Franjevački put, and then turn left up Alkarska. After the church is the monastery, which dates from 1614.

Trogir's patron saint, watched over by statues of Mary and Christ, the Apostles and saints. As you leave, note the Renaissance **baptistery**, to the right of the main portal, attributed to 15th-century sculptor Andrija Aleši. Inside, above the altar, note an unusual relief of St Jerome (Jerolim) and the Cave.

Trg Ivana Pavla II

Opposite the cathedral stands another masterpiece by Aleši, the **Čipiko Palace**, which has fine Venetian-Gothic windows. The wooden figure of a rooster in the entrance was taken from the prow of a Turkish ship at the Battle of Lepanto in 1571.

The **15th-century loggia** across the square from the Čipiko Palace used to house the Hall of Justice. The stone table where the judges sat is still there, as is a relief depicting Justice and the two patron saints of Trogir on the wall behind. In contrast to these Renaissance works is the Modernist equestrian relief by Ivan Meštrović on the back wall.

Fish Market

Leave the main square by Ulica Kohl-Genscher, to the right of the loggia. Follow this cobbled street to arrive at a second city gate, on the seaward side of town, dating from 1593. To the left stands a **16th-century loggia** that now serves as a fish market. From here you have views across to the island of Čiovo, which is now a suburb of Trogir accessible by bridge. Proceed right along the seafront, past the white neo-Gothic school building, and on the right is **Fontana**, see ①①, which makes a good restaurant stop.

Kamerlengo Fortress and Marmont's Pavilion

Continue along the seafront to reach **Kamerlengo Fortress** (summer 9am–8pm; free) which was built by the Venetians in the 1400s as part of the city's fortification system. In the summer it doubles up as an open-air cinema.

On the western tip of the peninsula stands a small neoclassical gazebo known as **Marmont's Pavilion**. Marshal Marmont, Napoleon's right-hand man during the time of the French occupation (1805–15), used to play cards and watch the sun set here on summer evenings.

MAKARSKA

Leave Trogir and return to Solin on the D8, then follow signs for the A1 motorway. Go southeast in the direction of Split and continue as far as Zadvarje, where you should follow signs south to the coastal road and

---

Food and Drink 🍴

① FONTANA

Obrov 1, Trogir; tel: 021-884 811; www.fontana-trogir.com; 9am–midnight; €€

Rare is the hotel restaurant that's worth a detour on its own merits, but the Fontana is one of them. Grilled fish and seafood are the main specialities, but there's also an assortment of meat dishes as well as a mixed vegetable platter.

② STARI MLIN

Prvosvibanjska 43, Makarska; tel: 021-611 509; daily 11am–midnight; €€

As it is about a five-minute walk from the seafront, there's a good price-quality ratio in this local place. Fish is the speciality and the ambience is casual.

Makarska  (90km/56 miles from Trogir). Once in the centre you will find the picturesque Old Town built around a naturally protected bay, backed by the awe-inspiring Biokovo Mountain.

In the 15th century, while cities such as Split and Šibenik were protected by Venice from Turkish invasion, this stretch of coast fell to the Turks. The Ottoman conquerors made Makarska an important administrative centre and fortified the town with walls and three towers that sadly no longer exist.

Kačićev Trg

Begin your tour on the seafront (Obala Kralja Tomislava), where **Hotel Biokovo** *(see p.113)* has a pleasant terrace bar in one of the best locations in town. Head along the palm-lined promenade until you see an opening on the left leading to **Kačićev trg** and the 18th-century Baroque **Church of St Mark** (Crkva sv. Marko). Around the square stand a number of fine Baroque town houses, built by wealthy merchants during the 17th and 18th centuries.

Road to Kotišina

Behind the church is an open-air **food market** (generally open mornings only), with steps leading up to the busy main road. Cross the road and take Makra put, which leads you over another busy road, and continue until you see a turning to the right, Mlinica put. This brings you to the small village of **Mlinice** (Little Mills), where there is indeed a semi-preserved complex of watermills. Follow this road and at the top you will find a mountain path and

a signpost to Kotišina. The 3km (2-mile) walk from Makarska to Kotišina takes about 40 minutes.

KOTIŠINA

Kotišina is a conglomeration of old stone houses that have been built into a craggy hillside. Following an earthquake in 1962, the entire population moved down to Makarska. Villagers now keep their former homes as weekend retreats, returning to cultivate small vineyards and olive groves. Upon arrival, look out for a wooden sign to the left that points to the **Botanical Gardens** (Botanički vrt). More giant rockery than formal garden, this place features a fine selection of clearly labelled indigenous plants and flowers.

Behind the garden, built into the cliff face, stands **Kaštel**. When the Turks conquered Makarska in 1499, the people of Kotišina defended themselves from this small fortress, which they had constructed to blend perfectly with the surrounding rocks. Above the windows, note the stone channels that were designed for pouring hot oil over the heads of attackers.

Return to Split

Return to Makarska's seaside promenade, with a choice of cafés, or head northeast to **Stari Mlin**, see ⑪②. Leaving Makarska, take the scenic D8 coastal road northwest and stop at the resort of **Baška Voda** ④. It is easy to park along the sea for a quick swim or a snack on the waterfront before returning to Split via the D8 (42km/26 miles).

Above from far left: Trogir's Cathedral of St Lawrence viewed through the 15th-century loggia; soaking in the clear coastal waters; seafood at Makarska seafront; the town sits below awesome Biokovo Mountain.

Biokovo Nature Park
Kotišina and the Botanical Gardens are part of the Biokovo Nature Park (Park Prirode Biokovo), a massive protected area that includes Biokovo Mountain and the network of hiking and climbing paths that lead to the highest point, sv. Jure at 1,762m (5,778ft). There are a number of protected species, including chamois goats and the moufflon (a wild short-fleeced mountain sheep), plus a variety of rare plants. To visit the park on your own, it is best to rent a jeep and start early. You can also arrange for organised hiking and jeep tours at Biokovo Active Holidays (Krešimira 7b; tel: 021-679 655; www.biokovo.net).

KRKA NATIONAL PARK AND ŠIBENIK

*Visit the splendid waterfalls, island monastery and traditional watermills of
Krka National Park. Afterwards, stop at Šibenik to admire the Cathedral of
St James, a World Heritage Site, and dine in an exquisite local restaurant.*

DISTANCE 158km (98 miles)
round trip; Krka boat tour
return trip: 32km (21 miles)
TIME A full day
START/END Split
POINTS TO NOTE
This tour should be done by car,
although it is possible by public trans-
port (take a bus to Šibenik from the
Split bus station, then at the Šibenik
bus station climb aboard a bus to
Skradin, the entrance to the National
Park). Bring warm clothes if you travel
upriver to Roški slap or Visovac, as it
can get cool in the late afternoon.
And bring your swimming gear.

The splendid network of lakes, cascades
and rivers that make up **Krka National
Park** (Nacionalni park Krka) are not
only a natural wonder, but form an
important part of Croatia's cultural heritage. There's an Orthodox monastery
far upriver, a Franciscan monastery and
the region's first hydroelectric plant.

Leave Split early and take the A1
motorway north 74km (46 miles) to
Skradin, which is located just to the
east of the motorway, at the mouth of
the River Krka.

KRKA NATIONAL PARK

The northern entry point to the Krka
National Park, **Skradin** ❶ has more
extensive facilities and resources than
the other entry, **Lozovac**, to the
south. The small town and marina
of Skradin comes alive with the
opening of the national park each
spring and then quiets down to
slumber as winter approaches.

The waters of the River Krka are
extraordinarily rich in fish, which
explains the town's long history.
Archaeologists have found traces of
habitation here from the Palaeolithic
era. It later became the Illyrian settlement of Scardona and then a Roman
municipality. Its location put Skradin
on a political fault line, and it passed
many centuries seesawing between
Croatian and Serbian rulers, and
Venetian and Turkish occupiers. The
1990s conflict was more of the same
for Skradin, which was badly damaged
in the conflagration. This was the front
line between the Croat-dominated
municipality of Šibenik and the inland
Serb-controlled area of Krajina. No
traces of conflict are visible now on the
quiet stone streets lined with prosperous shops and busy cafés.

Your first stop should be the **Krka National Park tourist office** (Trg Ivana Pavla II; tel: 022-217 720; July–Aug 8am–9pm, Sept–June 9am–8pm, www.npkrka.hr) in the big glass building on the main road, not to be confused with the small Skradin tourist office (Trg Mate Gospe 3; tel: 022-771 306) on the harbour. The national park tourist office will sell you an admission ticket and give you the schedule of boats running to Visovac and Roški slap *(see margin, p.67)*. There are a number of grocery stores in Skradin to pick up picnic supplies.

Skradinski Buk

Take a national park boat (included in park entry fee) to **Skradinski buk ❷** at the confluence of the green River Čikola and the blue River Krka. Here pay the fee at a small kiosk (if you have not already bought a ticket at the national park office in town), and take a narrow path that leads to a lovely grassy clearing surrounded by trees and overlooking the first series of waterfalls. It's a great place to picnic, and is also the only spot where swimming is allowed – in a roped-off area at a safe distance from the falls. Allow about 1½ hours to explore Skradinski buk, more if you intend to swim.

Nearby, a wooden footbridge takes you across the river. The disused hydroelectric power station on the right was one of Europe's first; it dates back to 1895 and the era when Šibenik was the first town in the Austro-Hungarian Empire to install electricity. Climb a flight of stone steps, make your way through the trees, past several stalls selling walnuts, dried figs and colourful bottles of fruit *rakija (see p.15)*, and, once you have reached the top, you will have a wonderful view of the waterfalls. Nearby, a renovated mill now houses a small **museum** that shows how local farmers used to bring their grain here to be milled while the women washed linen in the swirling waters.

Above from far left: *rakija* for sale at Skradinski buk; one of the park's waterfalls; reeds.

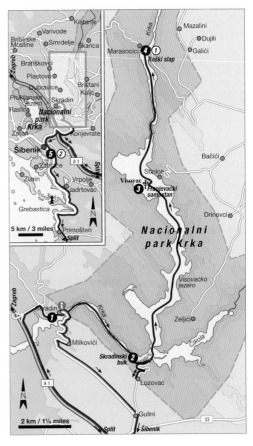

Above from left:
Cathedral of St James,
Šibenik; flowers in the
Franciscan Monastery
garden at Visovac; the
monastery bell tower.

Although the museum is interesting, you will probably find the network of falls and streams more eye-catching. Here, the River Krka plunges down 17 cascades with a total drop of 46m (150ft) and a width of 200m (665ft). To experience the full panorama follow the signs to **Lozovac**, the southern entrance to the park. The wooden walkways run through shady woods and over bubbling brooks for about 1km (²/₃ mile), and you will be treated to views of the falls from all angles.

Visovac

From Skradinski buk follow the signpost to the boat dock for the Visovac and Roški slap excursions *(see margin, right)*. The trip upriver is magical as the blue waters meet the steep, rocky cliffs.

Located 4km (2½ miles) from Skradinski buk, **Visovac ❸** is a tiny islet on which a perimeter of cypress trees shelters a 16th-century **Franciscan Monastery** (Franjevački samostan; www.visovac.hr). Even without the

stunning setting, the monastery would be worth a visit for the first printed edition of *Aesop's Fables*, dated 1487, exhibited in the monastery museum. Only two other copies of the book exist. Also in the museum are paintings, sacred objects and other rare books, and outside is a lovely flowering garden, tended by the monks.

Roški Slap

Boats stop at Visovac for about 20 minutes before continuing upstream to the park's most remote waterfalls, **Roški slap ❹**. The cliff walls seem to press in on you as the gorge narrows to a width of 150m (492ft). The 26m (84ft) high falls are bordered by watermills on the eastern side, and at the top of the falls is a restaurant, **Roški slap**, see ⑪①, with panoramic views. The visit includes time to explore the watermills. The boat will take you back to Skradinski buk, from where you can catch the boat back to Skradin (on the half-hour, 9.30am–7.30pm).

Leave Krka by late afternoon, then take the local road to Šibenik, 9km (5½ miles) southeast.

ŠIBENIK

The Old Town of **Šibenik ❺**, established by the Slavs in the 10th century, is built on a hill overlooking the Krka Estuary. Steep, narrow, winding streets lead from the seafront to a hilltop fortress. Like Skradin, Šibenik bounced back and forth among rulers and occupiers, and was attacked by Yugoslav forces in 1991, dealing a serious blow to

the local economy. Many people are still out of work and tourism is negligible, as Šibenik is one of the few coastal towns to find itself without beaches. But it does have the finest cathedral in Dalmatia, perhaps in all Croatia.

Cathedral of St James

The Old Town is closed to traffic, but there is a car park at the eastern end of the seaside promenade. Start at the harbour (in front of the car park or the bus station 100m/yds to the east), and walk along the seafront to find the **Cathedral of St James** (Katedrala sv. Jakova; summer 8am–8pm, winter 8am–noon and 5–7pm; free) up on the right. This building, erected between 1431 and 1536, displays a fine mix of late-Gothic and Renaissance architecture. Of the ornate Gothic portals, the main one, depicting *The Last Judgement*, is surrounded by the Twelve Apostles and crowned with a portrait of Christ; the side portal, depicting the *Entrance to Paradise*, is guarded on either side by a lion, one carrying Adam, the other Eve.

The cathedral adopted Renaissance characteristics in 1441 when Juraj Dalmatinac, who was born in Dalmatia and trained in Venice, proposed the addition of a transept and apses to form a Latin cross, topped with a magnificent cupola. He also created an extraordinary frieze running around the outer walls that portrays 74 heads of diverse figures, wearing turbans, kerchiefs and ribbons. These were probably the very faces that would have been seen in this coastal town. Unfortunately, Dalmatinac died before the building was finished. The completion of the roof, which is made up of monolithic stone panels, and the mounting of the splendid cupola, are attributed to Nikola Fiorentinac.

Inside, to the right of the altar, the delightful Dalmatinac-designed **baptistery** was actually created by the sculptor Andrija Aleši. The stonework of this semi-underground cavern is carved as finely as lace, creating a marvellous sense of light and energy in a tiny space. As you leave, check out Ivan Meštrović's statue of Dalmatinac to the right of the main entrance.

By now, you may be ready for dinner, in which case you might try the excellent **Gradska vijećnica**, see ②, just across from the cathedral.

Back to Split

If you have time, take the coastal road to Split for the scenery, especially the view of **Primošten**, a tiny town crowded onto a peninsula. Otherwise, just hop back on the motorway for the 75km (46½ miles) back to Split.

Boat Trips in Krka

From Skradinski buk there are only two or three boats a day (depending on the season) that go further upriver. One boat takes you on a four-hour tour to Roški slap that includes a visit to Visovac. Another one or two boats make the two-hour trip to visit the Visovac monastery. There is an extra charge for these excursions, payable in Skradin or Skradinski buk. In order to do the tour to Roški slap from Skradinski buk, it's best to arrive at Skradin in time to take the 10am boat.

Food and Drink

① ROŠKI SLAP

Roški slap, Krka National Park; daily lunch and dinner; tel: 022-785 9975; www.roskislap.com; €
Surprisingly good local specialities are on offer here, and there may well be freshly caught Krka fish on the menu. However, the main attraction is the unforgettable view.

② GRADSKA VIJEĆNICA

Trg Republike Hrvatske, Šibenik; tel: 022-213 605; Mon–Sat 9am–1am; €€€
This fine restaurant is housed in one of Šibenik's most beautiful buildings, a 16th-century Venetian loggia that is now the Town Hall. From one of the outside tables, you can appreciate the view of the cathedral while feasting on expertly grilled scampi and fresh pasta.

VIS

A tour of idyllic Vis Island, taking in the fishing village of Komiža, Tito's Cave, the island's remote beaches and the historic town of Vis. Devote a second day to the unforgettable Blue Cave on Biševo Island.

DISTANCE 32km (20 miles)
TIME One or two days
START/END Vis Town
POINTS TO NOTE

You can reach Vis from Split by ferry or catamaran; but only from June to September do the boat schedules allow a day trip to Vis (for details see www.jadrolinija.hr). The rest of the year you must make it an overnight trip. Note that to visit the Blue Cave, you must arrive the night before. For accommodation options *see p.113*.

It's helpful to have wheels to visit Vis Island, but consider renting a car, bike or scooter when you arrive. The price for bringing a car onto a ferry for a day trip can be more expensive than renting a car on arrival, and queues to get on the ferry can be long. Try Ionios (Obala sv. Jurja 37; tel: 021-711 535) or Navigator (Setaliste Stare Isse 1; tel: 021-717 786; www.navigator.hr). If you don't have your own wheels, it's best to take the bus to Komiža that awaits the arrival of the morning ferry. In that event, visit Komiža first and Vis Town when you take the afternoon bus back. Note that the Archaeological Museum of Vis Town is closed 1–5pm and on Mondays.

Remember to bring swimming gear.

Below: snapshots of the island's coast and interior.

Two and a half hours by boat from the mainland, mountainous Vis Island is happy to get a stream of tourists in the summer and then equally happy to return to the main business of producing wine the rest of the year. The journey can be blissful on a fine day as the boat passes by Brač, Šolta and Hvar islands, before gliding into the wide harbour of Vis Town.

In World War II the Yugoslav Partisans established their headquarters deep in the island's forested interior. Vis later became a military naval zone that was closed to foreigners until 1989. Thus, not only is the land forested and unspoilt, but the sea is teeming with fish. The island is one of the most popular diving destinations in Croatia.

If you have your own wheels, you could visit Vis Town first. Otherwise, it is best to take the bus directly to Komiža. For information on bus times, see www.info-vis.net.

KOMIŽA

From Vis Town take the road to **Komiža ❶**, which is a scenic 9km (5½-mile) trip through the hilly interior. Your first view of Komiža is from the brow of the hill above town, where a spectacular panorama over the Adriatic opens up before you. The bus

drops you almost in the centre of town, one block back from the Riva (seafront promenade) and the main square, **Škor**. The old stone buildings and narrow cobbled streets face south towards the harbour, and are protected to the north by a dramatic range of steep, conical hills that are volcanic in origin.

St Nicholas Monastery

Above the town the **Monastery and Church of St Nicholas** (Crkva sv. Nikola) are well worth visiting. These were founded in the 13th century by Benedictine monks, who had settled on nearby Biševo Island two centuries earlier, but fled due to the ever-present threat of piracy. Every year on St Nicholas's Day (6 December), locals gather in front of the church to perform a ceremonial burning of a fishing boat.

On the road up to the church of St Nicholas, note a track to the right and the *plaža* (beach) sign. The path runs down to the coast on the town's eastern side, where you will find a series of rocky coves and secluded beaches, some of which are given over to nudism.

On the western side of town, just after Hotel Biševo, you will find another pebble beach and a bar. Nearby stands the 16th-century Renaissance **Church of Our Lady of the Pirates** (Crkva gospa gusarica), which, it was hoped, would protect the town from pirate attacks.

For lunch, try **Konoba Jastožera**, see ⑪①, in the centre of the harbour. After, if you have your own transport, it's time to explore the rest of Vis Island. Otherwise, catch the bus back to Vis Town.

VINEYARDS

Once you have passed the Church of St Nicholas, the road weaves along high cliffs with majestic views of the sea to the right. The road takes you through the vineyards that produce Plavac, Vis's excellent wine, and there are a number of wineries that are open to visitors. Around Podhumlje try **Cobo** ❷ (tel: 021-713 750), and near Podšpilje you will find **Vinarija Podšpilje** ❸ (tel: 021-715 054) among others.

Above from far left:
Komiža; Stiniva Bay has a lovely beach; Monastery and Church of St Nicholas; boat detail.

Food and Drink 🍴

① KONOBA JASTOŽERA

Komiža Harbour; tel: 021-713 859; daily lunch and dinner; €€
The dining room of this restaurant is built on planks above the sea and is sure to spark an appetite for seafood. Lobsters are its speciality, but all the fish and seafood is so fresh it practically wriggles on the plate. After your meal, ask for a glass of *rogačica*, a local spirit flavored with carob, which grows in abundance here.

TITO'S CAVE

Just before Podšpilje, a sign on the left directs you to Borovik, site of **Tito's Cave** ❹ (Titova špilja). It was in the midst of these forests that Tito and his Partisans took shelter from the Germans in a cave from June to October 1944. Tito coordinated many a significant military operation from this cave, and crucial meetings between the Partisans, the Yugoslav government-in-exile and the Allies were held here. A short hike up some steep steps takes you from the road up to the cave. There is not much to see, but it is a pleasant detour. Return to Borovik and

Below: Tito's Cave.

take the country road to the village of **Žena Glava** ❺, with great views of the island and sea. You may wish to stop for refreshment at **Pol Murvu**, a local *konoba*, if it is open. From Žena Glava, you can return to the main rroad.

BEACHES

Return to the main road and turn left. After a few kilometres, you will see a sign on the right directing you to **Stiniva** ❻. The unpaved road takes you to the top of a cliff overlooking Stiniva Bay. It is a steep scramble to the bottom, but the unspoilt beach at the foot of this stunning bay is worth the trouble. Make sure you have enough water, as there is nowhere to buy snacks or drinks at the bottom.

Back on the main road, continue east until a sign directs you to **Rukavac** ❼. Here there is another idyllic beach, **Srebena**, easily accessible via a path to the right of the small car park. The beach is rocky but lined with pine trees.

Take the main road heading north, and a few minutes later you will be back in Vis Town.

VIS TOWN

Vis Town ❽ (Grad Vis) was founded by the Greeks in the 4th century as Issa, and soon became a powerful city-state. Nevertheless, Issa lost its autonomy when the Romans took over in 47BC. In the Middle Ages there were two settlements – Luka to the west and Kut to the east – that today are

joined to form a continuous urban complex stretching 3km (2 miles) around the bay. At the entrance to Vis harbour is an islet with a lighthouse named after Captain Hoste, head of the British fleet based here during the Napoleonic Wars. At the northern end of the harbour is the Prirovo peninsula, where the George the Third fortress was built to protect Vis harbour.

Greek and Roman Ruins

From the town centre and ferry dock, walk north along the seafront for about 100m/yds until the commercial area ends and you come to the tennis courts. Turn left and walk behind the tennis courts to find remains of the **ancient Greek cemetery**, which lies right outside the walled town built by the Greeks. You can still see remains of the **Greek walls**. Return to the seafront and continue walking north along the coast. After a few metres, across from the petrol station, you will see the remains of the **Roman baths**.

Archaeological Museum

Now walk in the other direction along the waterfront, passing the ferry dock. About 100m/yds later, on your right, is the **Archaeological Museum** (Arheološki muzej; tel: 021-711 017; summer Tue–Sat 10am–1pm and 5–9pm, Sun 10am–1pm, winter Tue–Sun 10am–1pm; charge), which provides an excellent overview of Vis's fascinating history. The museum is lodged in an Austrian fort *(batarija)*, and contains one of Croatia's most extensive collections of Greek artefacts. The

star of the collection is the bronze head of Aphrodite, sculpted in the 4th century BC.

For dinner, the most outstanding choice in town is the **Vila Kaliopa**, see ⑪②, located near the museum.

Food and Drink

② VILA KALIOPA

Vladimira Nazora 34, Vis Town; tel: 021-711 755; daily 8am–2pm, 5pm–2am; €€€

This exquisite restaurant is set in the walled garden of a 16th-century villa. The menu is determined by produce available on the day, including an abundance of fish and seafood. The sophisticated dishes display an Italian influence, which appeals greatly to the swanky Italians who invade the place on summer evenings. You might wish to dress up.

The Blue Cave

Biševo Island, lying 5km (3 miles) southwest of Komiža, is nearly uninhabited, except for a few families still tending to vineyards. Yet each summer this tiny island becomes a magnet for excursionists on their way to the famous Blue Cave (Modra špilja). There are other caves embedded on the island's coast, but the Blue Cave is truly special. Through a narrow sea corridor, you will find yourself floating in a blue chamber 24m (78ft) long and 12m (39ft) wide, with translucent water shimmering beneath you. The cave is magical at any time, but the best time is between 11am and noon when a strong shaft of sunlight pierces the cave, reflects off the seabed and bathes the interior in an unearthly blue glow.

A number of travel agencies in Komiža organise day trips to Biševo, also including a few hours' bathing at Porat Bay (Porat uvala), one of the few sandy beaches on the east Adriatic. Try Alternatura (Hrvatskih mucenika 2; tel: 021-717 239; www.alternatura.hr). The excursion usually runs from 9am to 4 or 5pm. For considerably more money you can book a taxi boat, but the rough seas are often not conducive to a small boat.

HVAR

A tour of the island of Hvar, with its unspoilt coastline, fine wines and lavender fields. See fashionable Hvar Town, which features some of Dalmatia's most beautiful 16th-century buildings, then visit some of the island's most scenic towns and villages.

DISTANCE Walking tour: 1.5km (1 mile); driving, returning via the hill villages: 67km (41½ miles)
TIME One or two days
START/END Hvar Town
POINTS TO NOTE

This tour has two parts: a morning walk in Hvar Town and an afternoon driving tour of Hvar Island. With stops for sun and sea, either part can be stretched to a full day. Regular year-round ferries to Stari Grad on Hvar Island are run by Jadrolinija (www.jadrolinija.hr). Another option is to drive to Drvenik on the mainland and take a Jadrolinija ferry to Sućuraj and then drive to Hvar Town. Alternatively, you could take a passenger boat from Split directly to Hvar Town (see www.krilo.hr). Exploring Hvar Island is hard to do by public transport, although there is a bus from Stari Grad to take ferry passengers to Hvar Town. You can also hire scooters or bikes on the island. To avoid exploring in the heat of the day, try to be at the door when the first museum (the Arsenal) opens at 9am and finish when the last museum (the Franciscan Monastery) closes at noon. It is advisable that you call the konoba Humac to check its opening times.

Holiday Island
Tourism began in 1868, initially for convalescents. Hotels still follow the tradition of offering free accommodation if it snows; a rare event on this, one of Europe's sunniest islands.

Hvar Island is the sunniest spot in Croatia, receiving 2,724 hours of sunshine a year. Much of the island is lush and hilly, but there are fertile plains and an indented coastline. The eastern part of the island is much less developed and markedly more rural than the west.

HVAR TOWN

Entrancing **Hvar Town ❶**, with its elegant Renaissance churches and old stone buildings, is arranged around three sides of a picturesque harbour that is sheltered from the open sea by the scattered Pakleni Islands, and backed by a hilltop fortress. Under Venetian rule (from 1331 to 1797) Hvar became one of Dalmatia's richest towns. Venetian merchant ships en route to the Orient would call here, and the town soon established its own fleet. Prosperity brought culture, which, coupled with a pleasant climate, and plentiful local wine and fish, must have made for a good life.

Arsenal

Start at the **harbour**, which is packed with flashy sailing boats in summer. At the northern end of the harbour is the **Arsenal**. Through a large arched entrance spanning 10m (33ft), workers pulled Venetian warships across the

slipway and into the drydock for repairs. The original 13th-century building was badly damaged during a Turkish invasion in 1571; the reconstruction of the present building was completed in 1612.

The upper floor's **Arsenal Gallery** (Galerija Arsenal; tel: 021-741 009; summer 9am–1pm, 5–11pm, winter by appointment; charge) exhibits contemporary Croatian art, with an emphasis on Hvar artists. To the right of the entrance stands the *zvir* (beast), a wooden prow in the form of a dragon, taken from the Hvar city galleon following a famous victory over the Turkish navy at the Battle of Lepanto in 1571.

Theatre of Hvar

In the same building is the historic **Theatre of Hvar** (Hvarsko povijesno; closed for renovations). Opened in 1612, the theatre's tiny interior was redecorated in a neo-Renaissance style in the 19th century. This was the first theatre of its kind in Europe and, unusually, it welcomed all, regardless of social position. Theatre was not new to Hvar: in the 14th century miracle plays were performed in the square in front of the cathedral. These days, performances are restricted to special one-off events.

St Stephen's Square and Cathedral

Back outside you will find yourself on Hvar's main square, **Trg sv. Stjepana**, which was formed by filling in an inlet. At 4,500 sq m (around 48,500 sq ft), it is the largest piazza in Dalmatia, and certainly one of the most beautiful. Walk its length to visit the **Cathedral of St Stephen** (Katedrala sv. Stjepana; daily 9am–noon and 5–7pm; free). The monumental Renaissance façade stands in harmony with the elegant 17th-century bell tower. A previous cathedral was destroyed by Turkish invaders in 1571, prompting the construction of this Venetian-style cathedral. The cathedral treasury is displayed in the **Bishop's Palace** (Riznica; tel: 021-741 152; summer 9am–noon and 5–7pm, winter 10am–noon; charge) just next door.

Above from far left: Hvar Town's main square and cathedral; yacht in an island cove.

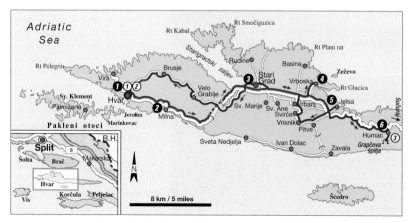

Above from left:
detail from the Franciscan Monastery's Renaissance cloister; Španjola citadel above town; Cathedral of St Stephen.

Only a few minutes' walk behind the cathedral is the **Summer Residence of Hanibal Lucić** (Ljetnikovac Hanibala Lucića; summer 9am–1pm and 5–11pm, winter 10am–noon; charge). Lucić (1485–1553) was a poet and playwright, and Hvar's most prominent citizen, whose romantic sensibility perfectly expressed his age. His Renaissance residence and gardens have been beautifully restored, displaying paintings and furnishings from the period.

Grad

North of the main square is Grad. Protected by the Španjola citadel, this was the aristocratic quarter, and still bears traces of the medieval palaces built after Hvar accepted Venetian rule in 1278. Grad is surrounded by 13th-century Romanesque walls, which are flanked by crenellated towers.

Take the street on the left as you face the cathedral, and take the first left onto Ulica Petra Hektorovića. Here you will see the city's oldest **well**, dating back to 1475, bearing a figure of the Venetian Lion holding a closed book, symbolising that Venice was at war at the time.

At the end of the street turn left to admire the unfinished 15th-century Venetian-Gothic **Hektorović House**, and then retrace your steps, going up the stairs to the **Benedictine Convent** (Benediktinski samostan; summer daily 9–11am, 7–9pm; free), an austere building with paintings, objets d'art and elaborate silk embroidery and lacework woven by the nuns, dating from the 16th to 18th centuries.

Španjola Citadel

Continue climbing the stairs and cross the road on top. Follow signs up to **Španjola**, the medieval citadel 90m (300ft) above sea level. Every Hvar ruling regime left its mark on the fortress, from the Venetians who strengthened it in 1557 to the Austro-Hungarians who added the barracks in the 1800s. Now it is a popular nightlife spot, **Veneranda**, with spectacular views. After a drink or an ice cream at one of the citadel cafés, if you have the energy you can continue the climb up to **Fort Napoleon** at 240m (786ft).

The Hotel Palace

Return to the town's main square, where the grand old Hotel Palace *(see p.113)* is on the right. The 17th-century Renaissance **city loggia** today serves as the hotel complex's reception hall. In front of the loggia is the **Štandarac**, a column from which all official decisions were announced in the 18th century.

Below: Sveti Klement, one of the Pakleni Islands.

Gojava Neighbourhood

Continue west along the harbour until you come to the **Nautika**, a popular bar at night. Turn right and you will come to the Church of St Mark, now a small **Archaeological Collection and Lapidarium** (Prirodoslovni kabinet Dr Grgur Bučic; tel: 021-741 009; summer 10am–1pm and 8–11pm; charge). If you feel like a swim, continue on the same road and after about 200m/yds you will come to the beach in front of the Hotel Amfora. Otherwise, return to the town centre and head south on Riva through the Burg neighbourhood.

Burg

In the 15th century the plebeians of Hvar began building their houses south of the main square on the Glavica hill, now the location of many of the private rooms and apartments to rent. Continue following the harbour until you come first to a tiny pebble beach and then to the **Franciscan Monastery and Museum** (tel: 021-741 193; summer 10am–noon and 5–7pm, winter 10am–noon; charge). The Renaissance cloister is exquisite and often hosts classical music concerts in the summer. The 16th-century bell tower is equally stunning, built by stonemasons from Korčula Island. The monastery church contains several notable works of art. Note especially the polyptychs by the Venetian artist Francesco da Santacroce, and sculptor Leandro Bassano's *Crucifixion* on the altar. Below the altar is the tomb of Hanibal Lucić. The monastery's rectory houses a museum, which is also a repository for priceless art, especially *The Last Supper* by an unknown 17th-century Italian painter and an edition of Ptolemy's *Atlas* from 1524. Notice also the unusual clock designed to toll the work cycles of the monastery rather than the hours.

Lunch Options

Walk back to town, where you can have lunch at **Hanibal**, see ①, situated on the square, or at **Bounty**, see ⑪②, on the other side of the port.

Food and Drink

① HANIBAL

Trg sv. Stjepana 12; tel: 021-742 760; www.hanibal.hr; daily noon–midnight; €€€

Pricey but delicious, this elegant restaurant is known for its sublime fish and seafood dishes, prepared with style and flair. Try the *brodetto* (fish stew) with polenta.

② BOUNTY

Fabrica bb; tel: 021-742 565; daily 10am–10pm; €€

In expensive Hvar, Bounty's fixed-price lunch menu is a relative bargain. The grilled fish, meat and pasta are correctly – if simply – prepared. Located on the western side of the harbour.

The Pakleni Islands

You can see the Pakleni Islands glittering just offshore in the midday sun, scattered like jewels on the Adriatic. Although the literal translation is 'Hell's Islands', in fact the name is probably derived from the word *paklina*, which is a special resin that was once used to coat ships. The island closest to Hvar is Jerolim, a favourite of naturists, although there are also 'clothed' beaches. Nearby is Marinkovac Island with Stipanska Beach. The largest island is Sveti Klement, famous for the gorgeous Palmižana hamlet. Here, gentle waves lap at a sandy cove ringed by pine trees. It is the Adriatic at its best. From Hvar Town, regular excursion boats make the run to one or more of the islands.

Stari Grad Plain

In 2008 Stari Grad Plain became the latest Croatian addition to Unesco's list of World Heritage Sites. Lying just a few kilometres east of Stari Grad, the plain still bears the ancient land divisions established by its original Greek settlers, as well as maintaining the same agricultural activities of vineyards and olive trees. It is possible to drive through the Stari Grad Plain by jeep east from Selo on an unpaved road, but it's even better to travel it by bicycle. The tourist office (tel: 021-765 763; www.stari-grad-faros.hr) in the town centre at Riva 2 has information about bicycle rental.

HVAR ISLAND

Milna

After lunch, head out of town towards Stari Grad. Take the 'new' road along the coast and make a stop at **Milna ➋**. This village sports two gravel beaches separated by a pine cove in a protected harbour, and offers a quiet respite from busy Hvar. Return to the road and continue on to Stari Grad.

Stari Grad

Now Hvar Island's principal ferry port, **Stari Grad ➌** is the oldest settled part of the island. Colonised by the Greeks in the 4th century BC, this rather workaday town bears few remnants of its illustrious heritage, although it is pleasant enough to stroll around the harbour. The most interesting sites are the **Dominican Monastery** (summer daily 10am–noon, 6–8pm; charge) and **Tvrdalj** (tel 021-766 324; summer daily 10am–noon and 6–8pm; charge), a castle that once belonged to Petar Hektorović, a renowned 16th-century poet whose most famous poem, *Fishing and Fishermen's Conversations*, is honoured by a fish pond within the walls.

Vrboska

Watch for the sign on the left on the road out of Stari Grad taking you to **Vrboska ➍**, Hvar's smallest town. At the end of a bay lined with pine forests, a narrow canal bisects the town, which is often called 'Little Venice'. Vrboska was founded in the 15th century, and a surprising number of houses remain from the 16th to 19th centuries. Immediately on entering the town you will notice the picturesque stone bridges lined by typical Dalmatian village houses to your right.

Cross the bridge ahead of you and walk to your left along the harbour. After about 50m/yds take the narrow alley on your right to come to the unusual **Church of St Mary** (Crkva sv. Marija; open for Mass only). Fearing attacks by the Turks, the villagers rebuilt the existing 15th-century church into a real fortress, which is unique in Dalmatia. From the top, there are sweeping views. Paintings from the Church of St Mary are currently on display in the nearby **Church of St Lawrence** (Crkva sv. Lovre; summer 10am–noon and 5–7pm).

Return to the main road, turn left and continue on to Jelsa, Hvar Island's other resort town. The journey takes you past a purple haze of perfumed lavender fields. Various herbs – lavender, rosemary, sage, marjoram and thyme – have been cultivated here since ancient times.

Jelsa

Although it may not have the glitz and glamour of Hvar Town, the small fishing town of **Jelsa ➎** makes a good

---

Food and Drink

③ KONOBA HUMAC

Humac; tel: 0915-239 463; summer Mon–Sat lunch and dinner; €€

Homemade food and drink from home-grown, home-brewed, home-caught or home-raised ingredients; you really can't get more traditional than this. There is no electricity here; the food is cooked on the barbecue or under a *peka (see margin, p.13)*. Call to before driving out as opening times can be somewhat unpredictable.

second choice for an island base. The buildings by the harbour date from the 19th century, when the shipping industry flourished. Call at **Villa Verde**, an appealing cocktail bar, for a drink on the Riva. From here visit the exquisite miniature Baroque **Church of St Ivan** (Crkva sv. Ivana; usually open in the morning, but times are irregular), one block back from the harbour. After a stroll around the **Old Town** at the foot of the harbour, you may wish to take the coastal promenade that runs from the southwest corner of the harbour and curves around the bay 400m/yds to the sandy **Mina cove**, a good place for a swim.

Humac

From Jelsa, return to the main road, and follow it the direction of Sučuraj (on the eastern tip of the island). **Humac ❻** lies 6.5km (4 miles) east of Jelsa. Look out for a wooden hand-painted sign on the right, then park the car off the road and walk the final 400m/yds along a track to arrive at this romantic cluster of semi-abandoned, traditional stone houses.

Humac was founded in the 13th century as a shepherds' settlement. In later years many inhabitants moved to the more sheltered and better-connected village of Vrisnik. For some years they returned to Humac to work the land, trekking three hours each way by mule or donkey. Today families from Vrisnik still cultivate these fields – keeping goats and growing vines, olives and lavender – more for pleasure than profit. Follow the old donkey

path up the hill behind Humac to arrive at the summit, which has great views of the south-facing slopes, the small island of Šćedro below and Korčula in the distance.

About 20 minutes from here on foot and signposted from the village lies **Grapčeva Cave** (Grapčeva špilja; free), a vast underground chamber of stalactites, stalagmites, halls and chambers.

Before leaving Humac, have dinner at the unique and unforgettable **Konoba Humac**, see ①③. Then return to Hvar Town by the same route; or, if you have time, you may wish to explore some of the island's hill villages *(see below)*.

Above from far left: moonlit Vrboska; lavender grows in the island's interior; breakfast at Jelsa.

Fešta Vina

Tipple a little at this renowned wine festival held in Jelsa on the last weekend in August.

Hvar's Hill Villages

From Humac, take the country road from Jelsa to Pitve, which was settled by the ancient Illyrians. From here, it is an easy drive to Vrisnik, another peaceful inland village. Return to the main road and head to Stari Grad. This time, take the country road that winds through the hills. Look for the sign on the left pointing you to Grablje and travel about 2km (1¼ miles) on an unpaved road to arrive at this nearly abandoned town with splendid views of the surrounding hills. Return to the main road and keep going until Brusje, an appealing clutter of stone houses only 5km (3 miles) northeast of Hvar Town.

DUBROVNIK

A full day in the beautiful city of Dubrovnik. An exploration of the main thoroughfare and city walls is followed by a visit to the city's museums and lunch by the Old Port. Afterwards, tour the cathedral and enjoy sunset drinks.

Patron Saint
In the 2nd century the Armenian bishop St Blaise (Sv. Vlaho) became a victim of Rome's anti-Christian purges. Some 800 years later, Blaise appeared to the rector of Dubrovnik Cathedral in a dream, warning of an imminent Venetian offensive, thereby helping to save the city. To mark the anniversary of his death on 3 February, a silver statue of the saint and relics of his body are paraded around town during an impressive religious procession.

> **DISTANCE** 3km (2 miles), including tour of city walls
> **TIME** A full day
> **START** Pile Gate
> **END** Synagogue
> **POINTS TO NOTE**
>
> Make an early start, as the walk around the city walls offers little shade: from noon onwards in summer it is extremely hot. This tour is intended as an introduction to the city; Dubrovnik has so much to see that to do it justice you really need more than one day.
>
> Dubrovnik is well connected by bus to other Croatian cities and by a twice-weekly ferry to the island of Korčula (www.jadrolinija.hr). There's also an airport south of town, but there are no trains to Dubrovnik. If you arrive by car, note that the Old Town is pedestrian only, but there is parking on the north, east and west entrances to the town.

Dubrovnik lies on the southeastern tip of Croatia. Dubrovnik's walled Old Town is small, with a circumference of a little more than 1.5km (1 miles). To the east of the Old Town is the Ploče neighbourhood, with several luxury hotels and residences; to the southwest lies the neighbourhood of Lapad, where most beaches and hotels are located; and to the northwest is Gruž, the harbour from where ferries run up the Dalmatian coast, as well as to the nearby Elaphiti Islands *(see p.85)*, Mljet *(see p.86)* and Korčula *(see p.92)*.

PLACA

Begin from the main entrance into town, **Pile Gate** ❶ (Pile vrata), approached over a wooden drawbridge on chains. The gate was constructed in 1537, with a Renaissance arch topped by a statue of St Blaise (Sv. Vlaho), protector of the city, displayed in a richly decorated niche. The inner gate displays a sculpture of St Blaise by the modern artist Ivan Meštrović *(see p.58)*. Once within the walls, you will notice a set of steep steps immediately to the left, giving access to the ramparts.

But first stroll along **Placa** (also called Stradun), the Old City's main thoroughfare, which was created when the channel that once separated Dubrovnik from the mainland was filled in. In the evening, this is where local people stroll before taking a seat at one of the pavement cafés, while their children eat ice creams and play.

The Baroque buildings along Placa are astonishingly uniform, each being of equal height and similar propor-

tions, with green-shuttered windows and space for shops on the ground floor. They were erected according to strict regulations following the 1667 earthquake; the harmonious arrangement of these buildings is a large part of Dubrovnik's architectural appeal.

Franciscan Monastery

At the Pile Gate end of Placa, the most striking monument is the circular **Onofrio Fountain ❷** (Onofrijeva česna), which still spouts fresh water. Built in 1438, the fountain is adorned with 16 carved masks. The water comes from a well 12km (7 miles) away, and

supplied residents with drinking water during the bombardment in 1991.

To the left is the entrance to the **Franciscan Monastery ❸** (Franjevački samostan; tel: 021-426 345; daily 9am–6pm; charge), a sober structure with a remarkable carving of the *Pietà* over the entrance that dates from 1498. The interior is known for its **cloister**, constructed in the mid-14th century. The capitals of each double column are topped with figures of people, animals and flowers, and the interior garden is fragrant with herbs and fruit trees. Also in the monastery is a **pharmacy** that has been dispensing natural and other

Above: Old Port with St John's Fort on the left and the arsenal on the right.

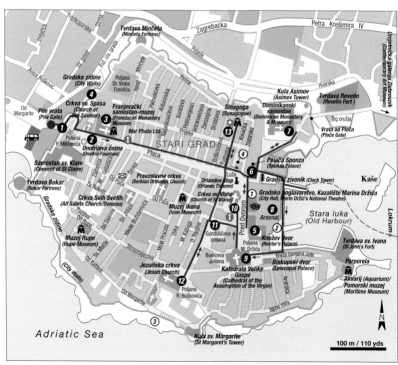

Historical Overview

After the Slavs ravaged the Roman city of Epidaurum (Cavtat) in the 7th century, the surviving inhabitants took refuge on an island, which they named Ragusa. The settlers built walls and the Republic of Ragusa was established in 1358, when Hungary granted the city freedom. The hinterland was rich in silver and lead, and Ragusa became the main port for exporting these materials. By the 1500s Ragusa had a highly respected merchant navy, and shipbuilding developed apace. In 1667, however, the city-state suffered a devastating earthquake which destroyed its Renaissance architecture and dealt it a severe economic blow.

The republic rebuilt; by the end of the 18th century and despite an economic recession, Ragusa had 673 ships and consulates in 80 cities. Yet it was in no position militarily to resist Napoleon Bonaparte's sweep of Europe. After 450 years of liberty, the Ragusa Republic fell to Napoleon in 1808, and after the French were expelled in 1813, became part of the Austro-Hungarian Empire until World War I. With the establishment of the Kingdom of Yugoslavia in 1929, the name Ragusa was dropped because it was deemed too Italian, and Dubrovnik took its place.

During World War II Dalmatia was occupied by the Italians. Croatian Nazis took control after the Italians were defeated in 1943 until Dubrovnik was liberated by Partisans. Under Tito, Croatia became one of six Yugoslav republics. Yugoslavia was more open than any other communist country and embraced tourism; by the 1960s tourism was Dubrovnik's major source of income, and in 1979 it was declared a Unesco World Heritage Site.

With the fall of communism, Croatia declared itself independent, a move supported by 94 per cent of Dubrovnik's population that was to have disastrous consequences. In December 1991 Serbian artillery shells began falling on the historic Old Town. Some 2,000 shells pummelled it until the bombing ended in 2002. Much of the city sustained serious damage, but thanks to substantial international assistance, Dubrovnik was able to replace and rebuild over the years. Its rebirth has been nothing short of astonishing.

concoctions since 1391; it is the third-oldest pharmacy in Europe. You might also take a look at the monastery museum, which displays a grab-bag of pharmaceutical equipment, relics, gold work, medical books and paintings.

Church of Our Saviour

Beside the monastery is the Renaissance **Church of Our Saviour** (Crkva sv. Spasa), built in 1520, in gratitude for the city's survival after a potentially destructive earthquake. Strangely, it was one of the few structures to withstand the earthquake of 1667. The acoustics of the church have made it a favourite concert venue.

CITY WALLS

The tour of the **City Walls ❹** (Gradske zidine; daily 8am–7pm; charge) can be commenced from the Pile Gate, from the equally imposing **Ploče Gate** (Vrata od Ploča) to the east, or from a third entrance by **St John's Fort** (Tvrđava sv. Ivana). In the days of the republic, the two main gates were ceremoniously locked at 6pm and opened at 6am the following morning. The tour will take at least an hour to complete, the circuit being about 1.5km (1 miles) long, with lots to see en route.

The fortification system dates back to the 13th century, although, as fear of foreign attack grew, the walls were further reinforced with additional towers and bastions. Cannons were positioned along the ramparts, and a deep trench was dug on the inland side. Note how the walls are much thicker

on the land side, as the city felt more vulnerable to attack by land than sea.

The views over the sea are idyllic, as are vistas over the city from any part of the walls. Remarkably, all the damage to the terracotta rooftops inflicted during the 1991–2 bombardment has been carefully repaired. The glossy new roof tiles are the only sign of the widespread damage and renovation.

When you have completed a circuit of the walls, return to Placa and make your way to Luža for Dubrovnik's imposing **Clock Tower** (Gradski zivonik), which first tolled the hours in 1444. On your right is the **Orlando Column** (Orlandov stup), sculpted in 1417 to honour the legendary Frankish knight Roland. His forearm was the official measure of the Ragusan Republic. Turning right you will come to the landmark **Gradska Kavana**, see Ⓨ①, on the left, a great place to take a break.

RECTOR'S PALACE

Next to Gradska Café is the **Rector's Palace ❺** (Knežev dvor; tel: 020-321 422; daily 9am–6pm; charge). The rector was a civic leader (with no ecclesiastical connection) chosen from the city's nobility. To avoid the concentration of power in one individual, a new rector was elected every month. He was obliged to reside here, and could leave only for official business.

The Rector's Palace was plagued by disaster: the original building was destroyed by a gunpowder explosion, the next one by fire, and the third by the 1667 earthquake. The present building, dating from 1739, is largely Baroque, although some Gothic details have survived, and there are some wonderful carvings on the capitals of the columns. At ground level, looking onto the courtyard, were official state offices, a meeting room and the jail (now part of the museum). At the far end of the courtyard stands a **bust of Miho Pracat**, a wealthy merchant who bequeathed one ton of gold to Dubrovnik, and to the left, below the stairs, a Gothic well. The official rooms upstairs looked over the town, while the rector's private quarters faced the harbour. Here you can see displays of period furniture and paintings, mostly Italian and Croatian works from the 17th and 18th centuries, and an unusual collection of clocks.

SPONZA PALACE

On leaving the Rector's Palace, cross over Placa to the **Sponza Palace ❻** (Palača Sponza; daily 10am–10pm; free). This is one of the few buildings that survived the 1667 earthquake, giving us some idea of what Dubrovnik architecture looked like before the quake. Built in the early 16th century,

Above from far left: Placa, the main thoroughfare; touring the city walls; handrail in the Rector's Palace.

A Divided City
Placa continued to divide the city even after the channel was filled. As late as the 16th century, the nobility lived in the area that was formerly the island, while commoners lived on the slope opposite, now Prijeko. Nobles were not allowed to flaunt their wealth by constructing ornate palaces: the rulers feared that the more the city displayed its prosperity, the more vulnerable it would be to attack. So the decoration of buildings was restricted to a family coat of arms above the main door.

Food and Drink 🍴
① GRADSKA KAVANA
Pred Dvorom 3; daily 8am–1am; €
From the raised terrace of this beloved café, you can spy on the Rector's Palace next door, the Church of St Blaise across the street and peek over at the entrance to the Sponza Palace to your right. It's a local favourite for the tempting array of ice cream and cakes on offer.

Summer Festival
Dubrovnik's Summer Festival (mid-July–mid-Aug) has become an increasingly prestigious way to catch the performances of the finest classical musicians, dancers and actors. Concerts and plays are held all around town; the most sought-after ticket is to the annual production of *Hamlet* on the terraces of Fort Lovrjenac. Find out more at www. dubrovnik-festival.hr.

it displays a combination of Renaissance and Gothic styles, typical of palaces built on the eastern Adriatic coast before the arrival of the Baroque tradition. In the time of the republic, the Customs Office was located here, hence the word *Dogana* ('Customs' in Italian) on the metal-studded door. One room in the palace has now become the **Memorial of the Defenders of Dubrovnik**, a moving dedication to those who died during the 1991–2 bombardment.

DOMINICAN MONASTERY

From the palace, take the narrow passage into the city walls. On the left is the **Dominican Monastery and Museum** ❼ (Muzej Dominikanskog samostana; tel: 021-426 472; daily 9am–6pm; charge), which contains Dubrovnik's most valuable paintings. The Domin-

ican monks took no chances with their treasure when, in the 14th century, they built their monastery to look like a fort. The interior is much more elegant, however, with a cloister that rivals that of the Franciscan Monastery. Cavtat artist Vlaho Bukovac (1855–1922) contributed a wonderful pastel of *St Dominic* in the monastery church, and Titian's *Mary Magdalene* (*c.*1550) in the sacristy is a must-see. Unsurprisingly, the church was a prestigious final resting place for Dubrovnik's noblest families. The monks also took it on themselves to support local artists, and the museum exhibits the apotheosis of the 15th- and 16th-century Dubrovnik school, with works by Nikola Božidarević, Lovro Dobričević and Mihajlo Hamzić. The triptych by Božidarević, showing Dubrovnik in the hands of St Blaise, is particularly interesting.

Right: Cathedral.

OLD PORT

Head to the Old Port on the east side of the town walls just behind the Rector's Palace. In the morning, small excursion boats to Cavtat, Lokrum and the Elaphiti Islands leave from here. If you feel like having lunch at this point, there are a number of restaurants on the port; the best is **Locanda Peskarija**, see ①②.

The Old Port is dominated by the arched entryways of the **Arsenal ❽**, where the republic's battleships were built and docked. From here you can see the **Lazareti**, on the coast to the left. This is where, in an effort to prevent the spread of infectious diseases, foreign sailors, travellers and merchants were held in quarantine. Today it is the venue for demonstrations of folk dancing during the summer (Tuesday and Friday 9.30pm).

DUBROVNIK CATHEDRAL

From the southern end of the Old Port turn right on Kneza Damjana Jude to reach the **Cathedral ❾** (Katedrala; Mon–Sat 9am–5.30pm, Sun 11am–5.30pm; free), a splendid example of 17th-century Baroque. A 12th-century Romanesque cathedral on the same site was partially funded (it is said) by England's King Richard (the Lionheart), as a token of gratitude for having survived a shipwreck near the island of Lokrum on his return from the Crusades in 1192. During restoration work in 1981, foundations of an even earlier church, dating from the

7th century, were discovered. The severe modern altar and arrangement of three seats for the clergy were designed to mirror the plan of the ancient church.

Treasury

The **Treasury** (Riznica) has a horde of richly decorated gold and silver reliquaries. Among the most precious pieces is the head of St Blaise encased in a gold Byzantine imperial crown embellished with precious stones. The saint's arm and leg are also on display. Most of these objects originate from the East, and arrived here courtesy of the Dubrovnik naval fleet.

CHURCH OF ST BLAISE

Follow the street in front of the cathedral until you reach the 18th-century **Church of St Blaise ❿** (Crkva sv. Vlaho; irregular opening hours; free). Named after the patron saint of Dubrovnik, the church overlooks Placa and is the frequent focal point of public events and celebrations. Built to replace an earlier church destroyed in the 1667 earth-

Dubrovnik Beaches
Dubrovnik is more than a treasured Old Town; it is also a place to relax by the beach and enjoy the pine-scented air. Dubrovnik's most popular beach is the sandy Copacabana Beach on the Babin Kuk peninsula. The shallow water makes it the best beach for children. Nearest to town is the gravel Banje Beach *(pictured)*, near the chic EastWest club. Much accommodation is on the Lapad peninsula, which also has a string of pebble beaches. The best is outside the Hotel Kompas. Another option is to take one of the many boats running to Lokrum just offshore. The island also has a number of naturist beaches that are clearly marked.

Food and Drink 🍴

② LOCANDA PESKARIJA

Na Ponti; tel 020-324 750; 11am–midnight; €€

With wooden tables on the Old Port, reasonable prices and friendly service, it's no surprise that Locanda Peskarija is a favourite of locals and visitors alike. Fish and seafood are the highlights here.

Above from left:
Lokrum island; hibiscus; morning fruit and vegetable market in Gundulić Square.

quake, St Blaise's ornate exterior is a fine example of Baroque style. Above the marble altar stands a silver figure of St Blaise that is paraded through the streets on 3 February each year *(see margin, p.78)*. The saint is portrayed holding a scale model of the city, providing one of the few records of what the city-state looked like before the 1667 earthquake.

Behind the Church of St Blaise is the pretty **Gundulićeva poljana** ⓫ (Gundulić Square), surrounded by old stone houses and dominated by a monument to Ivan Gundulić, the city's greatest poet. A colourful **fruit and vegetable market** is held here each morning; when it ends, the stalls are replaced by tables set up by a number of restaurants, and becomes a relaxing, casual spot in which to dine. Continue through the square and take the steps at the far end to the Jesuit Church.

Below: Jesuit Church.

JESUIT CHURCH

From the square, turn left and take the broad flights of steps up to the **Jesuit Church** ⓬ (Jezuitska crkva; daily 8am–6pm; free). Also called the Church of St Ignatius (Crkva sv. Ignacija), it is one of Dalmatia's finest examples of early 18th-century Baroque architecture, designed by the Jesuit architect Ignazio Pozzo, who modelled the interior on the Gesù Church in Rome. Next to the church is the Jesuit College, where many of the city's notables were educated.

PRIJEKO

Now return to Placa, cross over and take any of the 14 narrow uphill streets that run to the northern section of the city walls. These pretty stairways are cut by **Prijeko**, a long, straight street whose numerous restaurants and bars are located in the most popular – but not

Food and Drink

③ CAFÉ BUZA
Od Margarite; daily 5pm–1am
There's no better place to watch the sun set and contemplate the wonders of Dubrovnik than from this cocktail bar on the rocks. No food served.

④ DUNDO MAROJE
Kovačka bb; tel: 020-321 021; daily 11am–midnight; €€
Tucked away on a little side street, this restaurant has never lost its local appeal despite the waves of visitors crowding the outdoor tables. The fish and seafood dishes are prepared Dubrovnik-style and the black risotto *(crni rizot)* is the best in town.

the best – quarter for eating out. The tall, narrow dwellings in these streets are more humble than the palaces found on the other side of town. Try to duck into the **Synagogue** (Sinagoga; Žudioska 5; Sun–Fri 10am–8pm; charge), which is the oldest Sephardic synagogue in Europe. It also contains an intriguing little museum with ancient Torah scrolls and information about Dubrovnik's historic Jewish community.

SUNSET DRINK

A good way to finish the day is with a sunset drink at **Café Buza**, see ⑪③. Head to the southern walls and follow Od Margarite until you see the sign saying 'Cold Drinks'. Go through the hole in the wall and you will come to a bar with tables and chairs spread out on the flat rocks. If you are staying for dinner, try **Dundo Maroje**, see ⑪④.

MORE SIGHTS

With more time to spend, you could walk from the Ploče Gate, past Banje Beach and the Lazareti to visit the **Contemporary Art Museum** (Umjetnička galerija Dubrovnik; Put Frana Supila 23; tel: 021-426 590; Tue–Sun 10am–1pm and 5–9pm; charge). Alternatively, take a boat from the Old Port to the island of **Lokrum**, for a swim and a picnic under the pine trees. A slightly longer trip will take you down the coast to the lovely little port of **Cavtat**. All the boat trips are widely advertised on the quayside. You could also visit the **Aquarium** (Akvarij; tel:

021-427 937; Damjana Jude 2; Mon–Sat 9am–8pm; charge), set back from the Old Port in the walls of St John's (sv. Ivana) fort. Also here is the **Maritime Museum** (Pomorski muzej; tel: 021-323 904; summer daily 9am–6pm, winter Tue–Sun 9am–6pm; charge). For a vivid illustration of the horrors of the 1990s war, see the **War Photos Limited** gallery (Antuninska 6; tel: 021-326 166; www.warphotoltd.com; Tue–Sat, summer 9am–9pm, winter 10am–4pm).

Elaphiti Islands Day Trip

The Elaphiti archipelago northwest of Dubrovnik comprises 13 islands of which only three are inhabited: Koločep, Lopud and Šipan. The island closest to Dubrovnik is the diminutive and densely forested Koločep, whose two little settlements have a combined population of just 148.

Lopud is slightly larger with a population of about 300, but it was once a major port. In the 15th and 16th centuries Lopud had a fleet of some 80 vessels and a shipyard. Many wealthy men built summer villas here, but little remains. From the harbour turn left at the stone well and you will come to the dilapidated Knežev dvor (Rector's Palace); look out for the splendid 15th-century Gothic windows. Return to the harbour and beside an imposing church, you will see a sign for the now abandoned Grand Hotel. Take the path marked Plaža Sunj beside the Grand Hotel and follow it for about half an hour through fields of aromatic herbs until you come to one of the region's rare sandy beaches.

It's possible to visit Koločep and Lopud independently by taking a morning ferry to Koločep, visiting for an hour or so and then taking the next ferry to Lopud. Otherwise, take one of the organised tours that visit Koločep, Lopud and Šipan islands. See www.jadrolinija.hr for the ferry schedule and www.atlas-croatia.com for tour information. Boats leave from Gruž harbour.

13 MLJET

A one- or two-day excursion to lush Mljet Island replete with beaches, forests and dazzling scenery. Visit the two inland lakes and island monastery of the wooded National Park; walk and cycle along shady trails, and swim or kayak on the crystal-clear lakes.

Mljet History

Those ancient Greeks who came across this island called it 'Melita', which means honey. Was it because of the bees swarming in the forests, or because island life was sweet? Romans also made their way to the island and made Polače their headquarters, building a palace with baths. The Benedictines took control of the island in the 13th century, building their monastery in the middle of Veliko Jezero. It was only a matter of time before Mljet's powerful neighbour, Dubrovnik, extended its tentacles to grasp control of the island. Mljet became part of the Ragusa Republic in 1410.

DISTANCE Round trip, including boat tour: 9.5km (6 miles)
TIME One or two days
START/END Polače
POINTS TO NOTE

The G&V line catamaran *Nona Ana* (www.gv-line.hr) leaves Dubrovnik's Gruž harbour, west of the Old Town, at around 9am every day from June to September. Tickets go on sale at the dock one hour before departure. Alight at the second port of call, Polače, about 1¾ hours' journey away, not at the first stop, Sobra (unless catching the car ferry, *see p.89*). If you are staying overnight, contact the tourist board (www.mljet.hr) in advance to arrange accomodation in the pretty lakeside village of Babine Kuće or, failing this, in Pomena. And take a torch, as paths have no lights.

Food and Drink 🍴

① RESTAURANT MELITA

Otok sv. Marija; tel: 020-744 145; daily 10am–midnight; €€
Vegetables are fresh from the monastery garden, and eggs are fresh from their chickens. The dishes are simple but tasty, and the shady terrace dining room makes you want to while away the day here.

Mljet is an island of steep rocky slopes, dense pine forests and dramatic views. It is one of the few Dalmatian islands that was never ruled by Venice, which explains why no great towns were founded here. Indeed, Mljet has survived the centuries in a state of relative isolation. What it has lost in terms of grand architecture, however, has been more than compensated by the preservation of indigenous forests. Over 72 per cent of the island is covered with Aleppo pines, Umbrella pines, holm oak and *macchia*, making Mljet the most thickly wooded island in the Adriatic. Tourism is kept to a minimum; the inhabitants are committed to tending their olive trees, vineyards and fruit orchards.

Mljet National Park (Nacionalni park Mljet) on the island's western end protects 31 sq km (12 sq miles) of woodland and two inland seawater lakes. Legend has it that Odysseus stopped here on his voyage and stayed for seven years.

VELIKO JEZERO

Buy your park entrance tickets at the kiosk in the port of **Polače ❶** (if you are staying overnight the charge may be covered in the cost of your accom-

modation), and a bus will take you on a five-minute ride to **Pristanište** on the shore of **Veliko jezero** (Big Lake), actually a tidal expanse of salt water that lies with the national park.

For a leisurely look at Veliko jezero, take the path that runs along the lake 2km (1¼ miles) east to **Soline**, which is little more than a scenic scattering of houses on the lake.

A shorter path runs 500m/yds west to **Babine Kuće**, a small cluster of old stone houses with flowery gardens, overlooking the lake. Both places have private accommodation, but many devoted visitors return on an annual basis, so rooms can be difficult to find.

St Mary's Island

Return to Pristanište, where you can board a small boat (at 10 minutes past each hour; fare included in entrance price) that will take you out to the

Island of St Mary ❷ (Otok sv. Marija) in the middle of the lake. The church and remaining parts of the monastery on the island are Romanesque and date from the 12th century, but there were a number of 14th-century additions, and a lot of changes were made in the subsequent 200 years when it gained a Renaissance façade. After the monks abandoned the place in 1808, it fell into disrepair, and is now being renovated by the St Mary's Foundation, in conjunction with the Diocese of Dubrovnik, to which it was handed back in 1997 under the Law of Returned Property.

The church, an imposing single-naved structure, can be visited, but the monastery and cloister are still under wraps and closed to the public. However, the ground floor functions as the **Restaurant Melita**, see ⑪①, and it is an extremely pleasant place to have an early lunch.

Above from far left: Veliko jezero; oleanders bloom all over the island.

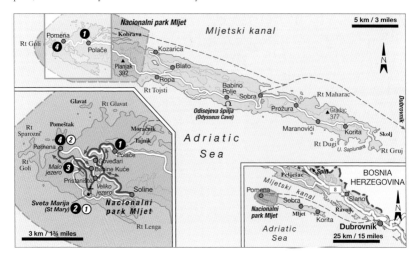

Exploring the Island

Before you eat, however, you might like to wander along the shady island paths. This stroll won't take more than about 15 minutes, even if you stop to visit the two little votive chapels, which were built by grateful sailors who had survived watery misfortunes. Alternatively, follow the coastal path for about 200m/yds from the monastery to find a good swimming spot from the rocky shore. If it is too early for lunch, treat yourself to a cool drink and an ice cream on the restaurant terrace, before getting the boat back to shore (45 minutes past each hour).

MALO JEZERO

The trip will not go directly to your starting point, but will take you to **Mali most** (Small Bridge) on the edge of **Malo jezero** ❸ (Small Lake), the second of the national park's lakes. Here, there's a small swimming beach and opportunities to rent kayaks, canoes and rowing boats, for those who would rather be on the water than in it. The water here is some 3 or 4°C (37–39°F) warmer than in the sea, so swimming is pleasant even in spring and autumn. Water enters the lakes through a narrow channel from the sea: if you stand at Mali most you

Below: lobster traps.

can see the water change direction with the tides.

A path, marked 'Pomena' – all the park's paths are clearly signposted – takes you round the side of Malo jezero on a pleasant path, easy underfoot, bordered by pines and olive trees, and with bright-yellow butterflies swooping along ahead of you.

POMENA

After a while the path leaves the lake and goes up a fairly gentle wooded hill, then descends to the little settlement of **Pomena** ❹. Once a tiny fishing village, it is now Mljet's tourist centre, albeit a restrained and pretty one. The **Hotel Odisej** *(see p.115)* dominates the bay. Some smart yachts bob in the water, and there are several modest restaurants, as well as the one attached to the hotel.

Follow a path round to the right of the harbour to find a row of little eating places. One, the **Galija**, see ❶❷, has lobsters in a huge brick tank on the terrace, so visitors can choose which one they want for lunch. There are more opportunities to rent bikes here. If you do rent a bike, be aware that you cannot bike all around Veliko jezero, but you can bike to the settlement of Soline.

POLAČE

To get back to Polače, return to Pristanište and follow the sign. Rather than taking the paved road that veers left, bear right and take the pedestrian path, Stari Put, back to town. Back in Polače, you could wander around the ruined walls of a Roman palace (the Romans founded Polače in the 1st century BC), but this won't detain you for long. Better to sit in one of the cafés that line the waterfront, enjoy the smell of wood smoke as restaurateurs fire up their barbecues, and try the local dessert wine, *prošek*, while you wait for the catamaran.

Above: Pomena, a popular yachting harbour.

Food and Drink
② GALIJA
Pomena; tel: 020-744 028; daily 10am–midnight; €€
A sweet little spot overlooking the sea and located opposite the Hotel Odisej. Rather expensive lobster is served here (along with many other places on the island), but there's lots of other, more reasonably priced, seafood and a few simple meat, pasta and vegetable dishes. Galija also has rooms to rent.

More of Mljet

Beyond the national park there lies a whole idyllic island, waiting to be discovered. You will need to have a car to do it justice though.

Take your car onto the ferry to Sobra (or rent a car from the Mini Brum agency at the Sobra port; tel: 020-745 084). From Sobra take the main road heading east. The route is extraordinarily scenic because of the indented coast and offshore islets. After about 45 minutes you will come to spacious Saplunara Bay and two stunning, sheltered sandy beaches lined by pine trees and shrubbery. There are a number of rare plants and very few people even at the height of the season.

As you make your way across the island to the National Park, stop in Babino Polje, the island's largest village. A sign, Odisejeva špilja, directs you down a steep path to Odysseus' Cave where the great wanderer supposedly met Calypso, daughter of Atlas. You could check out the 15th-century church of St Blaise (Sv. Vlaho) and the 16th-century Ducal Palace at the edge of the village.

PELJEŠAC PENINSULA

A one-day tour of the Pelješac wine-growing peninsula, Croatia's second-largest peninsula, including a visit to the Ston wall, swimming on Trstenica Bay, lunch in Orebić, winery visits and dinner at Mali Ston.

DISTANCE 226km (140 miles)
TIME A full day
START/END Dubrovnik
POINTS TO NOTE

This tour can only be done by car, as there are only one or two buses a day between Dubrovnik and Orebić. Start early in order to visit the walls of Ston while it is still cool.

Separated from the mainland by a narrow channel, the Pelješac peninsula is a sparsely populated, mountainous sliver of land 71km (44 miles) long and 7km (4 miles) wide at its maximum. The northeast part of the peninsula sprouts only *macchia*, but the southwest is car-

peted with fruit trees and vineyards that produce Pelješac's renowned Dingač and Postup wines. Equally renowned are the sandy beaches of the Pelješac peninsula, which are a rarity in Croatia.

STON

Leave Dubrovnik early in the morning and take the E65 coastal road to **Ston** ➊ (55km/34 miles). This appealing stone town is protected by a sturdy **wall** that winds up and around the surrounding hillside for 5km (3 miles), encircling Ston and neighbouring Mali Ston. In fact, the wall came before the towns. The Ragusa Republic *(see p.80)* annexed the region for its salt, and in the 14th century built walls to protect

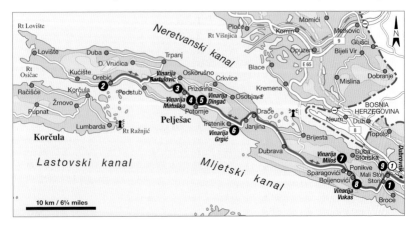

its investment and towns for the workers and guards involved in this huge engineering project. An irregular pentagon with massive corner towers fortifies the town, and the walls climb to the top of Pozvizd hill before descending to merge with the walls of Mali Ston. The wall system includes 40 towers and five forts. It's the longest fortification in Europe, and if you climb to the top you will be rewarded with sweeping views of the peninsula and the saltpans that are still in use today.

After your visit, you can take a break in one of the cafés sprawled along Ston's **central square**. While in Ston, you can pick up a free map of the Pelješac Wine Road at the tourist office (tel: 020-754 452) right at the entrance to the town, next to the car park.

OREBIĆ

Leave Ston and drive to **Orebić** ② (58km/36 miles), a rapidly developing coastal town with regular ferries across the channel to Korčula Island. Until the 19th century Orebić was a major maritime centre; now it is famous for the pine-lined beach along **Trstenica Bay** at the eastern end of the town, one of the finest beaches in Croatia. It has some snack bars, or you can walk along the coast towards town, where you will find a full line-up of restaurants and cafés.

WINERIES

After lunch and a look around town, head back east on the same road to visit some wineries *(see margin, right)*.

The first one you will come to is **Vinarija Bartulović** ③ (tel: 020-742 095) at Prizdrina. This 480-year-old winery is the only one that produces rosé. Next up is **Vinarija Matuško** ④ (tel: 020-742 393) in Potomje, which offers a chance to taste a full range of Pelješac wines. Back on the road, you will shortly come to the **Vinarija Dingač** ⑤ (tel: 020-742 010), also in Potomje, which is an agricultural co-operative that produces the venerable Dingač wine. Then it's on to the most famous (and expensive) winery, **Vinarija Grgić** ⑥ (tel: 020-748 090), at Trstenik, the Croatian branch of Grgić's California wine operation. **Vinarija Miloš** ⑦ (tel: 020-753 098) in Ponikve and **Vinarija Vukas** ⑧ (tel: 020-753 031) in Boljenovići are two further options before reaching Ston.

MALI STON

Pass through Ston, and after a short way turn left to the tiny walled village of **Mali Ston** ⑨. Croatians travel a good distance to feast on the seafood of Mali Ston. If you want to do the same, stop at **Kapetanova Kuća**, see ⑪①, before heading back to Dubrovnik.

Above from far left: saltpans at Ston; a plate of Mali Ston oysters; Ston's lengthy 14th-century wall.

Winery Practicalities The wineries on the peninsula are small family-run operations, so visits are relatively casual affairs. It's usually not necessary to call in advance if you come Mon–Sat 9am–noon or 2–6pm. Otherwise, advance notice is helpful. Note: the legal blood/alcohol limit for drivers is lower than the UK *(see p.106)*, so make sure you have a designated driver.

Food and Drink 🍴

① KAPETANOVA KUĆA
Mali Ston; tel: 020-754 555;
daily lunch and dinner; €€€
Right outside the town walls and on the bay, the owners have made the preparation of local seafood their life's work, with sensational results.

KORČULA

A one-day excursion to forested Korčula Island, famous for its olive oil and wine. Tour the turrets, towers and churches of walled Korčula Town, then relax on the sandy beaches of Lumbarda and taste the local Grk wine.

DISTANCE Driving: 230km (140 miles); walking: 1km (½ mile)
TIME A full day
START Sea Gate
END Large Governor's Tower
POINTS TO NOTE

In July and August there are regular morning catamarans (www.gv-line.hr) from Dubrovnik's Gruz harbour, west of the Old Town, that return in the afternoon. Tickets go on sale at the dock one hour before departure. The rest of the year you would need to hire a car, drive 115km (70 miles) to Orebić on the Pelješac peninsula, then make a 15-minute ferry crossing. You could then spend the night here and perhaps combine the trip with a visit to the Pelješac peninsula *(see pp.90–1)*. Once you have arrived at Korčula, be sure to check return ferry times.

Traces of Korčula's former Venetian overlords are readily apparent, from the ornate Renaissance flourishes on building façades to the paintings by Venetian artists in the cathedral. It remained under Venetian rule from 1420 to 1797, during which time the Venetians made good use of the local stone. Korčula was also an important shipbuilding centre. At their height, the island's shipyards rivalled those of Venice and Dubrovnik, and at the end of the 18th century there were still about 100 in operation.

KORČULA TOWN

Approaching Korčula by boat is unforgettable. As your boat nears the walled town, its four sturdy towers, honey-coloured walls and terracotta roofs resemble a fairytale city. Once in harbour you will see straight ahead of you a broad flight of steps, dividing around a central fountain. This is the **Sea Gate ❶** (Primorska vrata), one of two entrances to the Old Town. Before going in you may like to pop into the adjacent **tourist office** (Obala Franje Tudjmana; tel: 020-725 701), which is set in a splendid 16th-century loggia. The terrace of the **Hotel Korčula** next door is an inviting place for a coffee.

At the top of the steps is a broad terrace lined with café tables, and, straight ahead, a narrow alley (Ulica Dinka Miroševića) leads up to **Trg sv. Marka ❷** (St Mark's Square), where you will find the cathedral, the Treasury Museum and the Town Museum.

St Mark's Cathedral

Like most of Korčula's buildings, the Gothic-Renaissance **St Mark's Cath-**

edral (Katedrala sv. Marka; open daylight hours; free) is constructed from the mellow limestone that made the island – and its stone masters – prosperous and famous. The tower and cupola, dating from around 1480, are the work of Marko Andrjić, whose sons, Petar and Josip, worked on numerous prestigious buildings in Dubrovnik, including the Sponza Palace and the Rector's Palace. Flanking the main doorway are curly-maned lions and some rather lewd naked figures representing Adam and Eve. Above the door sits St Mark, robed as a bishop.

Inside, the cathedral is notable for a splendid high wooden ceiling; a huge stone canopy, also the work of Marko Andrjić, and built to his own design; and a richly coloured Tintoretto altarpiece (1550), depicting *St Mark with St Bartholomew and St Jerome*. In the south aisle there is an *Annunciation* that is ascribed to the School of Tintoretto; and in the north aisle there is Ivan Meštrovic's early 20th-century bronze statue of St Blaise (Sv. Vlaho).

Treasury Museum

To the right of the cathedral is the **Treasury Museum** (Opatska riznica; daily 9am–2pm, 5–8pm; charge). This elegant limestone building houses an eclectic array: its artworks range from 15th-century sacred paintings – including a precious polyptych of *Our Lady of Conception* by Blaz Trogiranin, one of the most respected 15th-century Dalmatian artists – to Ivan Meštrovic's 20th-century bronze *Pietà*. There are also ecclesiastical robes, chalices and processional crucifixes; and at ground level there's a cool kitchen, with large metal pots in the hearth and shelves stacked with Roman pots and jars of all shapes and sizes, that were recovered from the sea in the 1960s.

Above from far left: terracotta rooftops; harbour and Large Governor's Tower.

Above: look out for numerous little architectural flourishes on the town's buildings and walls.

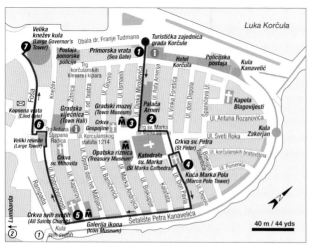

Sword Dances

Korčula is known for its festivals and its desire to keep traditions alive. The most important celebration is the Moreška, or Sword Dance Festival, held on St Theodor's Day (29 July), when lavishly dressed 'medieval knights' perform a stylised dance and play *(pictured on p.18)*. A shortened version of the dance takes place on an outdoor stage at the Old Town gate every Thursday in summer (ask at the tourist office for details).

Below: Marco Polo and the tower named after him.

Town Museum

Directly opposite is another museum worth visiting, the **Town Museum** ❸ (Gradski muzej; daily 9am–2pm, 5–8pm; charge), in a Renaissance palace built for the wealthy Gabrielis family in the 16th century. The ground floor has an interesting exhibition on the island's stonemasons; the first floor concentrates on Korčula's second important industry – shipbuilding – which utilised timber from the densely wooded island. Elsewhere in the museum are rooms housing 17th- to 19th-century furniture, elaborate costumes, portraits of the Andrjić family and kitchen implements. On the top floor, easily overlooked and not mentioned in the museum's guide, are photographs of Tito's Partisans, including one showing the First Conference of the People's Liberation Council for the district, held in November 1943, along with an old typewriter used by the Partisans.

Marco Polo Tower

Leave the square at the northern corner, taking Ulica sv. Roka. The first street on your right is Ulica Depolo, the alleged location of Marco Polo's birthplace. The building in question is a ruined but graceful Gothic palace, purchased by the town council in 2004 and undergoing renovation. You can visit the lovely **Marco Polo Tower** ❹ (Kuća Marka Pola; daily 9am–8pm; charge), entered through a pretty vine-covered patio, with stunning views from the top.

Now drop in to the nearby **Church of St Peter** (Crkva sv. Petra; summer daily 10–7pm; charge), a simple little chapel, and the oldest one in the town, where an exhibition portraying the life of Marco Polo is on display. This is pure kitsch: exhibits include cardboard cut-outs dressed in 13th-century robes, models made of shell and polystyrene depicting pirate ships, and a map on which the explorer's journey flashes in coloured lights.

Church of All Saints and Icon Museum

From the Church of St Peter take the steps down Ulica Don Pavla to Šetalište Petra Kanavelića and turn right. At the end of the road you will come to the **Church of All Saints** ❺ (Crkva svih svetih; usually open in daylight hours; free) in order to see a beautiful 15th-century polyptych by Blaz Trogiranin (whose work is also in the Treasury Museum). Across the way is the **Icon Museum** (Galerija ikona; daily 10am–2pm and 5–7pm; charge), housed in the Hall of the Brotherhood of All Saints. Painted on wood in tempera and gilt, some of the 17th- and 18th-century icons are truly exquisite.

Gates and Towers

Continue on Ulica Dobrotvornosti on the other side of the church and you will come to the majestic stone steps leading to the **Land Gate** ❻ (Kopnena vrata) to the town. On the left is the 15th-century **Large Tower** (Veliki revelin) and ahead is the **Town Hall** (Gradska vijećnica). Climb the tower for far-reaching views of the glistening sea and the coastline.

Afterwards go down the steps out of the Old Town and turn right, until you reach the cone-shaped **Large Governor's Tower** ❼ (Velika knežev kula). This was built at the western corner of the walls to protect both the Governor's Palace (now demolished) and the harbour. Turn left here, and follow the harbour road for a different view of Korčula and the chance to swim at one of two small bathing beaches. Alternatively, turn left at the steps, for the eastern port for the bar-café-restaurant **Marco Polo Mistique**, see Ⓨ①.

LUMBARDA

Korčula is more than just a town; there's a whole island to explore. If you have a car, you could take the main road to Vela Luka to explore the forested interior. But even without a car, it is worth taking a look at Lumbarda, 6km (4 miles) southeast of Korčula Town. There are hourly buses (make sure to check the return schedule at Korčula's bus station), or you could hire a taxi or a taxi boat from the eastern harbour on the way to the bus station. En route, you will pass acres of vineyards growing the Grk grape to make Lumbarda's renowned white wine.

Lumbarda itself is a pleasant and low-key small town on a harbour and endowed with the island's best beaches. Walk south out of town for 1km (²/₃ mile) to come to two sandy beaches: Pržina and Bilin Zal. The fine sand and shallow water make either one suitable for kids. On your return to Lumbarda you could sample some local wine at one of the harbourside cafés. Back in Korčula Town, you may wish to dine at **Konoba Barka**, see Ⓨ②.

Above from far left: the warm limestone of St Mark's Cathedral; Venetian lion on the Land Gate; Old Town view.

Food and Drink 🍴

① MARCO POLO MISTIQUE
Nova riva; tel: 020-715 432;
daily 8am–midnight; €€
This stylish spot on Korčula's eastern port serves up whatever you want, from coffee and cakes to full meals involving grilled fish and pasta. There's an outdoor terrace and an air-conditioned dining room.

② KONOBA BARKA
Od teatra 12; tel: 020-715 329;
daily noon–11.30pm; €€
Korčulans are justifiably proud of their special ways of preparing the wonderful local fish and produce. The outdoor terrace over the port provides a tranquil setting for sampling well-prepared dishes.

Marco Polo Connection

'Did he or didn't he?'... come from Korčula, that is. Most historians place Marco Polo's birthplace squarely in Venice (around 1254), but that convinces no one here in Korčula. 'But we have a Depolo family that goes back centuries', Korčulans will respond.

Wherever he was born, it is clear that the world's first guidebook writer is most fervently admired in Korčula. Note the hotel, restaurants and businesses named after Marco Polo. In late May there is even an annual festival called the Return of Marco Polo, when a suitably clad character is welcomed by the mayor and led to his home, where he entertains the townspeople with stories of his travels, before they all settle down to a concert of Renaissance music.

DIRECTORY

A user-friendly alphabetical listing of practical information,
plus hand-picked hotels, restaurants and entertainment venues,
clearly organised by area, to suit all budgets and tastes.

A

ADDRESSES

In Zagreb and Split, street names can be written two ways, in the nominative or possessive case *(see p.26)*. Occasionally, you will see the letters, 'bb' which stands for *bez broja* (without number). It indicates that there is no numbering on the street. In small towns such as Hvar and Korčula, street names either do not exist or are rarely used. Other than that, the names and numbering of addresses are as you would expect.

C

CHILDREN

Croatia has plenty of beaches, which makes the coastline a great place for family vacations. In Istria, Poreč has the widest assortment of family-friendly hotels with a full range of outdoor activities for kids to enjoy. Dubrovnik's Copacabana Beach on the Babin Kuk peninsula has a beach playground, and the shallow waters are safe even for toddlers.

Croatians are generally children-friendly. While few restaurants have high chairs for toddlers, there is a casual dining atmosphere and getting children's meals is rarely a problem. Kids get discounts everywhere; in museums, at hotels and on ferries. The vast array of apartments for rent along the coast can keep costs down for family travel.

CLIMATE

The best time to visit Croatia is during spring and summer, when days are sunny and dry. Coastal temperatures regularly reach 30°C (86°F) in August. The Croatian coast is significantly warmer than its interior. In January, temperatures in the east of the country can fall al low as -1°C (30°F) but can be as high as 10°C (50°F). In Istria, autum, although mild, is often wet.

CLOTHING

Although dress is casual in Croatia, locals tend to be neat dressers, and women pay close attention to fashion trends. The 'grunge' look never made much headway in Croatia. Restaurants rarely require a jacket and tie, but it is wise to pack a sports jacket for the more upmarket establishments. Many young Croatians dress to impress at night; anyone wishing to go to fashionable bars or clubs would be wise to do the same. In spring and autumn, it is best to be prepared for rain and the occasional cooler temperature, but summers are hot, even at night, so you are pretty safe if you pack only lightweight clothing. November to March can be cold, so bring a warm coat.

CRIME AND SAFETY

Croatia is relatively safe, but you should take the normal, sensible precautions: be especially careful when withdrawing money from ATMs; hold

tight to your belongings in markets and other crowded places; and avoid any unsalubrious areas at night, especially if you are alone.

CUSTOMS

Coming into the country, duty-free allowances for visitors are (per person): 1 litre of spirits, 2 litres of wine, 200 cigarettes or 50 cigars. Do not be alarmed by random 'everybody off' spot-checks at the border when travelling by train or bus: these searches tend to be for smuggled black-market goods.

D

DISABLED TRAVELLERS

The organisation that handles the needs of the disabled in Croatia is Savez Organizacija Invalida Hrvatske (Savska 3, Zagreb 10000; tel: 01-482 9394). Most – but not all – large hotels are wheelchair-accessible, and usually public toilets in major cities are too. Public buses and trams are usually not wheelchair-accessible. Most local ferries have elevators. See www.jadrolinija. hr for more details on wheelchair-accessible ferries.

E

ELECTRICITY

The electrical current is 220 volts AC, 50Hz. Most sockets have two round pins. UK visitors should pack an adaptor (available from airports, large chemists' stores, supermarkets, etc.) for appliances brought from home. US visitors will need a transformer for 110-volt appliances.

EMBASSIES AND CONSULATES

Embassies and Consulates in Croatia

Australia: Centar Kaptol, Nova Ves II; tel: 01-489 1200.

Canada: Prilaz Đure Deželica 4, Zagreb; tel: 01-488 1200.

New Zealand: Vlaška ulica 50a, Zagreb; tel: 01-461 2060.

UK: I. Lučića 4, Zagreb; tel: 01-600 9100;

Vukovarska 22, Dubrovnik; tel: 020-324 597;

Obala hrvatskog narodnog preporoda 10/III, Split; tel: 021-341 464.

US: Thomasa Jeffersona 2, Zagreb; tel: 01-661 2200.

Croatian Embassies and Consulates

Australia: 14 Jindalee Cres, O'Malley, Canberra; tel: 02-6286 6988.

Canada: 229 Chapel St, Ottawa; tel: 613-562 7820.

New Zealand: 131 Lincoln Road, Henderson, Auckland; tel: 09-836 5581.

South Africa: 1160 Church St, 0083 Colbyn, Pretoria; tel: 012-342 1206.

UK: 21 Conway St, London; tel: 020-7387 2022.

US: 2343 Massachusetts Ave NW, Washington, DC; tel: 202-588 5899; www.croatiaemb.org.

Above from far left: autumn colours in Plitvice; Franciscan Monastery, Hvar; Grožnjan.

Further Reading

The Death of Yugoslavia by Laura Silber and Allan Little. A detailed analysis of the break-up of Yugoslavia and its descent into civil war.

A Nation Forged in War by Marcus Tanner. A readable history of Croatia from the arrival of the Slavs through to the 1990s.

Yugoslavia as History by John Lampe. Highly recommended analysis of the two Yugoslavias, and why they didn't work.

Black Lamb Grey Falcon by Rebecca West. Fine account of a journey through Yugoslavia in 1937.

Dubrovnik in War edited by Miljenko Foretić. Various authors examine different aspects of the Homeland War. Contains numerous black-and-white photographs.

EMERGENCIES

Police: 92
Fire brigade: 93
Ambulance: 94
Road assistance: 987

G

GAY TRAVELLERS

Homosexuality is legal in Croatia but not fully accepted. Openly gay venues are non-existent largely because of prejudice from the local populations. Discos and bars in major cities such as Zagreb and Dubrovnik are usually gay-friendly, but public displays of affection are frowned upon. On the last Saturday in June, Croatia's LBTG population comes out of the closet and flocks to Zagreb's Gay Pride Day. The rest of the year, gays head to naturist beaches to meet others, but note that these are not exclusively gay beaches.

H

HEALTH

No vaccinations are required to enter Croatia and there are no particular health issues in the country. Tap water is safe to drink everywhere.

Medical Services

There are reciprocal healthcare agreements between most EU countries and Croatia, entitling such citizens to free medical care, although payment is required for prescribed medicines. UK nationals need only show a passport to receive free care. However, in order to cover all eventualities (including repatriation), it is advisable to take out private travel insurance before leaving home.

If your country does not have an agreement with Croatia, you will have to pay according to listed prices. Most doctors speak some English. In an emergency go to *hitno pomoć* (casualty).

Pharmacies

Pharmacies are open Monday–Friday 8am–7pm, Saturday 8am–2pm. The following are open 24 hours:
Zagreb: Ilica 43, tel: 01-484 8450.
Split: Dobri, Gundulićeva 52; tel: 021-348 074; and Lučas, Pupačićeva 4; tel: 021-533 188.
Dubrovnik: Two pharmacies alternate weekly. In the Old Town, Ljekarna Kod Zvonika, Placa; tel: 020-428 656; and, near Gruž harbour, Ljekarna Gruž, Gruška obala; tel: 020-418 990.

HOLIDAYS

Banks, post offices and most shops close on public holidays.
1 Jan: New Year's Day
6 Jan: Epiphany
Late Mar or early/mid-Apr:
Easter Sunday and Monday
1 May: May Day
22 June: Anti-Fascist Day
25 June: Statehood Day
5 Aug: National Thanksgiving Day
15 Aug: Assumption Day
8 Oct: Independence Day
1 Nov: All Saints' Day
25 and 26 Dec: Christmas

HOURS

Banks. Most banks are open Monday–Friday 7am–7pm, and some open on Saturday 7am–1pm.

Churches. These are generally open 8am–noon and 4–7.30pm, although some stay open all day from July to August, while others have more irregular hours. Remote churches only open for their respective saint's days.

Food shops. Most food shops are open Monday–Friday 7am–8pm, Saturday 7am–1pm. The majority of towns have at least one food store open on Sunday morning, but a recent law mandating Sunday closings may mean that this is not to be counted on. Food markets are only open in the morning.

Museums. Most museums open 9am–noon; in summer many stay open in the afternoon, and in the resorts some open in the evening in peak season. Dubrovnik's museums generally open 9am–6pm in summer. Some museums close on Sunday, others on Monday.

Local tourist offices. Local tourist offices have three seasons: winter, shoulder and summer season. In the winter, hours are regular business hours, that is Monday to Friday from 8 or 9am to noon or 1pm and then from about 2–5pm. In the shoulder season (May, June, September) hours are extended to Saturday morning. In July and August hours are long, often from 8am to 8pm daily.

Post offices. Most post offices are open Monday–Friday 7.30am–7pm, Saturday 8am–1pm.

Shops. Along the coast, clothes shops, bookshops, museums and the like close for a long lunchtime siesta. Their opening times are roughly Monday–Saturday 8am–1pm and 4–7pm.

L

LANGUAGE

The official language is Croatian, a Slav tongue written in Latin script. Each region has its own dialect. Zagreb and the north borrow from German; Istria and Dalmatia use Italian expressions. Istria has a large Italian minority, and some street signs are in both Croatian and Italian. A number of towns have names in both languages, which can be confusing for visitors.

Local dialects can also be confusing when reading a menu: the names of some dishes, especially fish meals, may vary from area to area. Most young people speak some English.

Below is some basic vocabulary. You will find more included on the pull-out map that accompanies this book.

Useful Words and Phrases
Hello *Bog*
Goodbye *Do viđenja*
Good morning *Dobro jutro*
Good day *Dobar dan*
Good evening *Dobra večer*
Good night *Laku noć*
Yes *Da*
No *Ne*
Please *Molim*
Thank you *Hvala*
Where is...? *Gdje je...?*

Pronunciation
Croatian vowels are not too difficult for English speakers, but consonants can be tricky:
c – ts as in 'bats'
č – ch as in 'cheese'
ć – ch as in 'future'
d – j as in 'jeans'
dz – dj as in 'adjust'
j – y as in 'yes'
lj – ly as in 'billion'
nj – ny as in 'canyon'
s – sh as in 'push'
z – zh as in 'measure'

Is there...? *Ima...?*
There isn't... *Nema...*
I would like... *Zelim*
Entrance *Ulaz*
Exit *Izlaz*
Open *Otvoreno*
Closed *Zatvoreno*
WC *Zahodi*
Men *Muškarci*
Women *Zene*

M

MAPS

City bookshops sell road maps. The Tourist Board publishes an excellent free map, and many local tourist offices provide useful, detailed town maps. Also handy are the Insight Fleximaps to the Croatian Coast and Dubrovnik, laminated for durability and easy folding.

MEDIA

Newspapers. In summer foreign newspapers and magazines are available in all the main resorts.

Radio. During the tourist season, *Hrvatska Radio 2* (Radio 2), on 98.5 MHz, broadcasts a brief news round-up in English (from UK Virgin Radio) every hour after the main headlines. The same station broadcasts traffic reports and nautical news several times daily in English, German and Italian.

Television. There are two state-run television channels and two privately run channels: Nova and RTL. Films are normally shown in their original language with Croatian subtitles.

MONEY

Cash machines. Banks in large towns and resorts have ATMs. Look for the *bancomat* sign.

Credit cards. All hotels, many restaurants and most shops accept the major credit cards: American Express, Diner's Club, MasterCard and Visa. Small *konobe* in out-of-the-way villages are not usually equipped to accept credit cards and if you stay in private accommodation, you must pay in cash.

Currency. The Croatian kuna (officially abbreviated as HRT, but most commonly written as Kn) is divided into 100 lipa. Foreign currency can be imported and exported freely. Anything up to 15,000Kn can be exported. The exchange rate is fixed and varies by season. Although the euro is not official currency, hotel room prices are often quoted in euros.

Traveller's cheques. The only reliable place to cash traveller's cheques is at an authorised change place, *Mjenačnica*. The exchange rate on traveller's cheques is generally not as favourable as the rate on cash or what you get withdrawing from a cash machine.

P

POLICE

Croatian police wear dark-blue uniforms and are generally helpful and friendly; many speak some English.

Anyone involved in a road traffic accident is legally required to report it to the police. In an emergency, dial 92.

POSTAL SERVICES

The Croatian postal service (www.posta.hr) handles mail quickly and efficiently. Stamps for international mail must be purchased at post offices, which are open from 7.30am to 7pm weekdays and from 8am to 1pm on Saturday. In addition to selling stamps, post offices also sell mobile phones, SIM cards and prepaid cards. Do not expect post office personnel to speak much English.

S

SMOKING

Recent legislation has banned smoking in all public places, including bars and cafés. It remains to be seen whether the puffing habits of Croatians will change, as cigarette-smoking is relatively widespread. Smoking is discouraged in hotels and private accommodation, although only the more expensive hotels have dedicated no-smoking rooms.

T

TELEPHONES

To call Croatia from abroad, dial 385.

Direct international calls can be made from blue public phone booths on the street with a phonecard available from newspaper kiosks. Or you can call from an HTP cabin (Croatian Telecoms), and pay when you have finished. Calls are cheaper between 7pm and 6am.

Dial 00 to call abroad, followed by the country code (UK: 44; Canada & US: 1; Australia: 61), then the number you wish to reach, omitting any initial zero.

International operator: 901
International directory inquiries: 902
Local directory inquiries: 988

Mobile phones. Croatia is on the GSM 900/1800 frequency, which means that most American mobile (cell) phones are not compatible. A Croatian mobile with a SIM card costs about 200Kn. A SIM card alone costs 100Kn, if you have a compatible phone. You can buy a mobile or SIM card at some post offices or the shops of Croatia's main providers: T-Mobile and Vipnet.

In Croatia, numbers that begin with 09 are mobile phones and are billed at a higher rate.

TIME DIFFERENCES

Croatia is one hour ahead of GMT: if it is noon in London, it is 1pm in Zagreb. Daylight saving is used.

TIPPING

Tips are not usually included on bills. Locals usually round up to the nearest whole number, but no one will object if you add on more. Consider that salaries for waiting staff are low and hours are long.

TOILETS

Croatia has standard Western toilets. Public toilets often require payment of 2Kn to the toilet attendant.

Above from far left: Diocletian's Palace column detail and peristyle, Split; Croatian police car.

TOURIST INFORMATION

The Croatian National Tourist Board and all the local tourist boards publish reams of information and maps that can be invaluable in planning your trip.

Tourist Information Offices

Croatian National Tourist Board (Zagreb): Ilberov Trg 10/4, Zagreb; tel: 01-469 9333; www.croatia.hr.

Zagreb City: Trg Bana Jelačića 11, Zagreb; tel: 01-481 4051; www.zagreb-touristinfo.hr.

Plitvice Lakes National Park: Plitvička jezera; tel: 053-751 015; www.np-plitvicka-jezera.hr.

Istria County: Forum 3, Pula; tel: 052-452 797; www.istra.hr.

Pula: Forum 3; tel: 052-214 201; www.pulainfo.hr.

Poreč: Zagrebačka 9, Poreč; tel: 052-451 293.

Rovinj: Obala P. Budicina, Rovinj; tel: 052-811 566; www.tzgrovinj.hr.

Pazin: Franine i Jurine 14, Pazin; tel: 052-622 460; www.tzpazin.hr.

Motovun: Šetalište V Nazora 1, Motovun; tel: 052-681 642.

Grožnjan: Ulica Gorjan 3, Grožnjan; tel: 052-776 131.

Split: Peristil bb; tel: 021-342 606; www.visitsplit.com.

Trogir: Trg Ivana Pavla II 1, Trogir; tel: 021-881 412.

Makarska: Obala kralja Tomislava, 16 Makarska; tel: 021-616 288.

Krka National Park: Trg Ivana Pavla II 5, Šibenik; tel: 022-217 720; www.npkrka.hr.

Šibenik: Fausta Vrančića 18, Šibenik; tel: 022-212 075; www.sibenik-tourism.hr.

Vis: Šetalište Stare Isse 2, Vis; tel: 021-717 017; www.tz-vis.hr.

Komiža: Riva bb, Komiža; tel: 021-713 455; www.tz-komiza.hr.

Hvar: Trg sv. Stjepana 16, Hvar; tel: 021-741 059; www.tzhvar.hr.

Dubrovnik: Dubrovačkih branitelja 7, tel: 021-427 591; Obala S. Radića, tel: 417 983; Obala pape Ivana Pavla II 44, tel: 417 581; www.tzdubrovnik.hr.

Mljet: Polače; tel: 020-744 041; www.np-mljet.hr.

Tourist Offices Abroad

UK: 2 The Lanchesters, 162–164 Fulham Palace Road, London W6 9ER; tel: 020-8563 7979; www.croatia.hr.

US: 350 Fifth Avenue, Suite 4003, New York 10118; tel: 212-279 8672.

Croatian Angels

This is a service that has been set up to assist visitors. For general tourist information, between 1 April and 31 October, tel: 062-999 999 (+385-62-999 999 if calling from abroad). The service is available in English, Italian, German and Croatian.

TRANSPORT

Arrival by Air

Croatia's national airline, **Croatia Ailines** (www.croatiaairlines.com), operates direct scheduled flights from London Heathrow Airport to Zagreb, Split, Dubrovnik and Pula. Flying time from London is just over two hours. In summer, the timetable is extended to include flights from Manchester to Split, Dubrovnik and Pula. The company also operates flights from most other principal European cities, but has no direct lines from the US.

British Airways (www.britishairways.com) flies from London Gatwick to Dubrovnik. Budget airlines include easyJet (www.easyjet.com) from London Gatwick to Split, Ryanair (www.ryanair.com) from London Stanstead to Pula and Zadar, Wizzair (wizzair.com) from London Luton to Zagreb, and Flybe (www.flybe.com) from Birmingham to Dubrovnik and Split.

The following airlines also fly to Croatia: Air France, Alitalia, Aeroflot, Austrian Airlines, ČSA (Czech Airlines), JAT (Serbia Airlines), LOT (Polish Airlines), Lufthansa, Malev and Turkish Airlines.

From April to September, it is possible to find cheap charter flights. These normally fly to Split, Dubrovnik and Pula.

To and from the Airport

Croatia Airlines runs a bus service to and from Zagreb airport to Zagreb Centre, with departures every 30 minutes. In Split and Dubrovnik, airport buses leave 90 minutes prior to the plane's take off, while buses from the airport leave shortly after the plane's arrives. For further information about airport bus links, contact: Zagreb (tel: 01-633 1999), Split (tel: 021-203 119), Dubrovnik (tel: 060-305 070).

Arrival by Road

To enter Croatia by car you require a green insurance card, which should be supplied by your rental company if you are hiring a car. The main road into the country from Western Europe is the E70, bringing you from Trieste, Italy, to pass through Slovenia for border crossings south for Istria and Dalmatia, or east for Zagreb.

Arrival by Train

There are train services direct to Zagreb from Italy, Slovenia, Austria, Hungary, Serbia, Bosnia-Herzegovina, France, Germany and Switzerland. The daily Eurocity 'Mimara' service runs from Munich, through Austria, to arrive in Zagreb via Ljubljana. Intercity trains run from Venice, Trieste, Vienna, Budapest and Belgrade.

For timetable information and booking tickets, contact Rail Europe, tel: 08448-484 064; www.raileurope.co.uk. For details of travelling from London to Croatia by train, see www.seat61.com.

Arrival by Sea

You can get to Dalmatia by ferry from Italy. Year round, **Jadrolinija** (tel: +385-51-666 111; www.jadrolinija.hr), the Croatian national ferry company, runs regular services from Ancona to Split and Zadar, and from Bari to Dubrovnik. The Bari-based Azzurra Line (tel: +39-080-592 8400; www.azzurraline.com) has a full summer schedule of ferries from Bari to Dubrovnik. Another Croatian company, **Blue Line** (tel: +385-021-338 292; www.bli-ferry.com), also covers the Ancona–Split route and

Above from far left: national football team merchandise. The team reached the 2008 Uefa Championship quarter finals.

runs summer ferries from Ancona to Vis and Hvar.

To travel to Istria from Italy (mid-July–mid-Sept), take Ustica Lines (tel: +39-040-303 540; www.usticalines.it) from Trieste to Rovinj or Poreč, or Venezia Lines (tel: +39-041-242 4000; www.venezialines.com) from Venice to Pula, Rovinj or Poreč.

Getting Around

Bus. A comprehensive coach network connects all parts of the country and is extremely reliable. Coaches can get busy in summer, though, so it is wise to pick up your ticket in advance at the bus station. Tickets cannot be purchased online. For times, contact Zagreb main bus station (tel: 060-313 333; www.akz.hr).

Taxi. Taxis are available in all major towns and resorts. Drivers are obliged to run a meter.

Driving. The coastal road is full of twists and turns, but the views are amazing. It is very well maintained but can be slow going in the height of summer, although there is also a motorway that runs along the coast to just south of Split.

The police are quick to catch speeding motorists, which can result in on-the-spot fines. The speed limit in towns is 50kmh (30mph); out of town it is 80kmh (50mph); and on motorways 130kmh (80mph). For cars towing caravans or trailers it is 80kmh (50mph). The blood alcohol limit is 0.5 per cent. Driving under the influ-ence can lead to severe fines and the confiscation of your licence. Tolls are payable on a number of motorways, and for passage through the Učka Tunnel between Rijeka and Istria.

Finding parking spaces in the coastal towns can be difficult, especially during peak season, as all central parking spots are reserved for residents with permits. If you abuse local parking restrictions, you risk having your vehicle towed away.

Another disadvantage of travelling by car arises when it comes to 'island hopping'. Vehicles frequently have to queue for hours before boarding ferries. Taking a car on a ferry can also be expensive; it may be cheaper and easier to rent a car once you reach the island and can decide if you need it. Also be warned that, if you are driving during the winter months, especially in the mountains, winter tyres are essential, and in extreme cases snow chains have to be used.

Hrvatski Autoklub (Croatian Automobile Club) provides a 24-hour breakdown service (tel: 987; www.hak.hr).

Car rental. There are services in all main towns, tourist resorts and airports. In addition to local car-rental companies, global companies such as Avis, Budget and Hertz are well represented. The web reservation service Economy Car Rentals (www.economycarrentals.com) works with local suppliers and often has the best deals.

Drivers must be over 21 years old and have held a valid driving licence

for a minimum of two years. A credit card and a current passport or national identity card are also required for car hire.

Motorbike. The coastal road from Istria down to south Dalmatia makes a fantastic trip for bikers. What's more, with a motorbike you can reach the more remote villages on the islands, without having the trauma that car drivers experience of waiting for hours to board ferries. (Bikes tend to queue-jump and are waved straight on.)

Ferry. Jadrolinija operates a coastal line from Rijeka down to Dubrovnik, stopping at Split, Stari Grad (Hvar), Korčula and Sobra (Mljet) en route. Misleadingly called *brze linje* (fast line), this journey is in fact extremely slow. But it does not really matter unless you are in a great hurry: the sea and the islands are beautiful, and comfortable cabins and a surprisingly good restaurant make this a truly memorable trip. Jadrolinija is also the main operator for the dozens of local ferries that connect the island with the coastal ports of Dubrovnik, Makarska, Split, Zadar and Rijeka. The winter schedule runs from October to May; the summer schedule from June to September. Services are more frequent and more expensive in the summer.

There is also a private company, **Krilo** (tel: +385-021-872 877) that runs a passenger boat connecting Split, Hvar and Korčula all year, and another, **G&V** (tel: +385-020-313 119; www.gv-line.hr) that connects Dubrovnik with Polače (Mljet Island), the Elaphiti Islands and Korčula (summer only).

Train. Rail travel is limited, but **Hrvatske Željeznice** (Croatian Railways; tel: 060-333 444; www.hznet.hr) runs a slow, comfortable overnight service, with sleeper compartments, between Zagreb and Split via Zadar and Šibenik. A quicker way to reach the coast is to take one of the two high-speed trains that connect Zagreb to Split in 5½ hours. There is no rail line to Dubrovnik. A good daytime service runs between Zagreb and Rijeka, passing through the beautiful forests of Gorski Kotar.

V

VISAS AND PASSPORTS

EU passport-holders and US, Canadian, Australian and New Zealand nationals do not need visas and can stay for up to three months.

W

WEBSITES

Visit the tourist office site (www.croatia.hr) for an overview; Croatia Traveller (www.croatiatraveller.com) for travel planning; and the Croatian homepage (www.hr) for useful links. For private accommodation, try www.adriatica.net, www.adriagate.net and www.atlas-croatia.com, which also organises excursions and ferry bookings.

Croatia's hotels are often sprawling structures, built during the tourist boom of the 1970s. However, in the last few years many have become part of hotel chains and have undergone major overhauls. The hotel scene is definitely upwardly mobile with more four and five-star hotels opening each year.

Hotel categories use the standard international grading system. Prices (posted in rooms) vary according to the season and are up to 50 per cent less off-season. For stays of less than three days you may have to pay a 30 per cent surcharge. Prices are posted in euros; you may pay in kuna or euros if you pay in cash. If you pay by credit card, the card will be billed in kuna at the prevailing exchange rate. Breakfast is almost always included in the price.

Zagreb

Arcotel Allegra
Branimirova 29; tel: 01-469 6000; www.arcotel.cc; €€€
The lobby of the Arcotel Allegra sparkles with colour, and the rooms include satellite TV, a DVD player, minibar and internet port. With its combination of comfort, design and superb location opposite the train sta-

Price for two people sharing a double room in peak season:	
€€€€	over 220 euros
€€€	160–220 euros
€€	90–160 euros
€	below 90 euros

tion, it is not surprising that the hotel is a favourite of business travellers.

Hotel Dubrovnik
Gajeva 1; tel: 01-486 3512; www.hotel-dubrovnik.hr; €€€
Clad in mirrored glass, the three-star Hotel Dubrovnik may be a monster to look at, but the location, just off Trg Jelačića, is perfect. Many of the rooms have a view of the square, and the double-glazed windows allow you to appreciate the view without being disturbed by the noise. The hotel attracts many anglophones, possibly because Zagreb's English-language bookstore, Algoritam, is part of the hotel building.

Hotel Ilica
Ilica 102; tel: 01-377 7622; www.hotel-ilica.hr; €€
This friendly hotel was one of Zagreb's first to cater to budget travellers. It started out in a small older building and spread to include the renovated building next door. Rooms are individually decorated and of different sizes, so you may wish to see a few before settling on one. The hotel is just a 15-minute walk west of the main square and right at a tram stop. There is also free hotel parking.

Ravnice
I. Ravnice 38d; tel: 01-233 2325; www.ravnice-youth-hostel.hr; €
A most cheerful 30-bed hostel with shared rooms (2–10 beds) and facilities, a 20-minute walk east of the centre. The hostel is easily reached by tram and the neighbourhood is quiet. Efficiently

run by an Australian expat, the amenities include a kitchen, a TV common room, laundry and internet access.

Regent Esplanade

Mihanovićeva 1; tel: 01-456 6666; www.regenthotels.com; €€€€

Built in 1925 for passengers of the Orient Express, the illustrious Esplanade stands next to the station. The swirl of marble in the lobby gives a taste of the classical splendour of the rooms. The high ceilings and fine tapestry are traditional, but the facilities are most modern and include a wellness centre, WiFi access, and Zinfandel's, a first-class restaurant (see p.32).

Plitvice

Hotel Jezero

Velika Poljana; tel: 053-751 400; www.np-plitvicka-jezera.hr; €€€

A large modern hotel renovated to include an indoor pool and sauna; comforts that can be most soothing in Plitvice's cold winters. All rooms are bright and plushly decorated, but try to get one with a balcony and a lake view. The hotel is open all year round.

Hotel Plitvice

Velika Poljana; tel: 053-751 132; www.np-plitvicka-jezera.hr; €€

This is a very comfortable hotel, although the rooms are not quite as expensively fitted out as those at the Hotel Jezero next door. Still, there is ample heat or air-con depending on the season, plus in-room satellite TV with English-language channels and a well-stocked minibar. No pool.

Istria: Poreč

Hotel Hostin

Rade Končara 4; tel: 052-408 800; www.hostin.hr; €€

This is a relatively new entry on the Poreč hotel scene, and was built to accommodate individual travellers rather than those on package tours. The rooms are smartly furnished, and facilities include pool, sauna and Jacuzzi. Hostin is set among pine trees near the bus station, a 10-minute walk from the Old Town. Open all year.

Hotel Neptun

Obala M. Tita 15; tel: 052-400 800; www.valamar.com; €€

If you are more interested in the cultural attractions of Poreč than the beaches, you might prefer to stay in town. The refurbished, three-star Neptun, on the promenade overlooking the sea and port, enjoys the best central location. The cheerfully decorated rooms have double-glazed windows to keep out any noise.

Hotel Poreč

Rade Končara 1; tel/fax: 052-451 811; www.hotelporec.com; €

This comfortable low-cost hotel next door to the bus station is a great favourite with backpackers and budget travellers, which lends the hotel a most convivial atmosphere. Despite the reasonable prices, rooms are well-maintained and spacious, bathrooms are large and modern. It is only a 10-minute walk to all the attractions of Poreč.

Zagreb Hotels
Unlike hotels along the coast, the prices of Zagreb hotels stay the same year-round. Many hotels cater to business travellers and tend to fill up during fairs and conferences. You may find better deals in summer.

Hotel Valamar Diamant

Brulo bb; tel: 052-465 000; www.valamar.com; €€€

Another link in the quality Valamar chain, this vast modern hotel has excellent sports facilities that include indoor and outdoor swimming pools and 16 tennis courts with instructors and equipment rental. There is also an impressive health and beauty centre. Just a 20-minute walk from the Old Town and open all year round.

Istria: Rovinj

Hotel Adriatic

P. Budicin 2; tel: 052-804 100; www.maistra.com; €€

If you just need a comfortable place to sleep after a full day of sightseeing in Rovinj, this three-star hotel is for you. The decoration may not be eye-popping, but the central location overlooking the harbour more than makes up for it. Enjoy breakfast on the terrace as you watch the fishing boats come in.

Hotel Katarina

Otok sv. Katarine; tel: 052-804 100; www.maistra.com; €€€

This large hotel is on St Katherine's Island, just a short shuttle boat away from central Rovinj. It is a great family

hotel because there are a wealth of facilities to keep kids occupied, such as the outdoor pool, tennis courts, diving and surfing schools, and playroom. There is also free internet connection. The hotel is open from April to October.

Hotel Park

I. M. Ronjgova bb; tel: 052-804 100; www.maistra.com; €€€

This large hotel is great for pampering. There are indoor and outdoor pools, a fitness centre, sauna and massage parlour plus a wealth of beauty treatments. Rooms are attractively but not imaginatively decorated. As it is only a 10-minute walk along the seafront south of centre, it is easy to pop into town to enjoy Rovinj's charms.

Villa Angelo d'Oro

Via Švalbe 38–42; tel: 052-840 502; www.rovinj.at; €€€€

A luxury hotel occupying a restored 17th-century building in the Old Town. The design is imaginative but still respects the traditional setting. All the rooms are individually furnished with antiques but also contain spacious modern bathrooms with all the trimmings. The facilities include a Jacuzzi, sauna and solarium.

Istria: Pazin

Laura's Guesthouse

Antuna Kalca 10a; tel: 052-621 312; €

This guesthouse provides extremely good value for money. The comfortable rooms are small but decorated, not merely furnished, and many have

Price for two people sharing a double room in peak season:	
€€€€	over 220 euros
€€€	160–220 euros
€€	90–160 euros
€	below 90 euros

terraces with a view of Pazin's castle. The castle, the Abyss and town centre are all an easy walk from the guesthouse. Breakfast is not included, but it is worth paying extra for it. The Pazin tourist office (www.tzpazin.hr) handles reservations.

Above from far left: Villa Angelo d'Oro; large hotels' facilities often include wellness centres.

Istria: Pula

Hotel Histria
Verudela; tel: 052-590 000; www.arenaturist.hr; €€€

Although built for mass tourism decades ago, this hotel on the Verudela peninsula has been extremely well maintained. The full resort experience includes several large saltwater pools, a wellness centre and the opportunity to indulge in a variety of water sports, such as water-skiing, scuba-diving, banana boats etc. There are also a number of restaurants and bars here, ranging from casual to more formal.

Hotel Riviera
Splitska 1; tel: 052-211 166; www.arenaturist.hr; €

This late 19th-century establishment has a lot of character. Rooms and bathrooms are immense, although the furnishings are standard issue. The high-ceilinged rooms need renovation, but there is a shady terrace just made for relaxing after a day of sightseeing, and the location – a few minutes' walk from the Arena – is perfect.

Hotel Scaletta
Flavijevska 26; tel: 052-541 025; www.hotel-scaletta.com; €€

For a little more style in the centre of town, try this attractive family-run hotel. Rooms are somewhat small, but the cheerful decor makes up for the lack of space. The tastefully restored town house is also situated just a stone's throw from the Arena.

Hotel Valsabbion
Pješčana uvala IX/26, Medulin; tel: 052-218 033; www.valsabbion.net; €€€

This lovingly constructed and furnished boutique hotel is known throughout Croatia for its award-winning restaurant (see pp.118–19), but it is also a rather wonderful place to stay. Overlooking the sea, 4km (2½ miles) from the city centre, it offers a beauty centre and hydro-massage pool, plus a fitness centre where you can work off any extra weight gained from over-indulgence at the table.

Istria: Livade

Istarske Toplice
Sv. Stjepana 60; tel: 052-603 410; www.istarske-toplice.hr; €€

This is Istria's best-known spa, whose thermal waters are renowned for their quality and therapeutic properties, and have been enjoyed since the Roman era. The resort is surrounded by woods and parkland, and although the rooms are bland, the facilities make up for it. Choose from the outdoor thermal pool or an indoor pool long enough to swim laps in. Special wellness packages include massage, mud baths, beauty treatments and the like.

Taxes and Charges
There is a 'tourist tax' charged on every stay, whether you stay in hotel or private accommodation. The tax is per person and per night, but it varies according to the location and the season. It runs between about 2.20Kn and 7Kn.

Central Dalmatia: Split

Hotel Jadran

Sustjepanski Put 23; tel: 021-398 622; www.hoteljadran.hr; €€

Sometimes it is more restful to stay a little out of central Split. This 1970s hotel overlooks Zvončac harbour, close to St Stephen's Gardens, and is just a five-minute walk along the seafront to the town centre. The hotel has been fully renovated to include a spa and fitness centre, and the rooms are bright and comfortable.

Hotel Peristil

Poljana kraljice Jelene 5; tel: 021-329 070; www.hotelperistil.com; €€

This is an excellent-value hotel spectacularly located in Diocletian's Palace. Only some rooms have a view of the peristyle, but all are in mint condition with air-conditioning, satellite TV and sparkling bathrooms. Some also incorporate parts of the ancient walls. Despite the active location, the hotel has been thoroughly soundproofed and the interior design is most soothing. The multilingual staff are professional and attentive.

Hotel Zephyrus

Miliceva 5; tel: 021-396 162; www.zephyrus.hr; €€€€

Price for two people sharing a double room in peak season:

€€€€	over 220 euros
€€€	160–220 euros
€€	90–160 euros
€	below 90 euros

There has long been a need for a luxury hotel in Diocletian's Palace, and the Hotel Zephyrus has amply fills that gap. With an upmarket style that caters to an international set that expects the best, this is a 'design hotel' with every room offering a different experience from classical Dalmatian to sleek and modern.

Le Meridien Lav

Grljevacka 2a, Podstrana; tel: 021-500 500; www.starwoodhotels.com; €€€€

It was a proud day when this five-star hotel, the region's best and one of Croatia's finest, opened in 2007. Podstrana is about 8km (5 miles) south of town, but Le Meridien Lav is a complete resort with spa, casino, restaurants, pools and beach. Naturally, there is a full wellness centre ready to pamper you with massages, aromatherapy, healing treatments, saunas and Jacuzzi.

Central Dalmatia: Trogir

Villa Pape

Marinova Draga 30; tel: 021-460 410; www.villa-pape.com; €

The English-speaking owners of this family-run establishment go out of their way to make guests feel welcome, offering a variety of services from airport transfers to personal guides. The excellent home-cooked meals use only local ingredients, which makes it worthwhile to take half-board. With modern, comfortable, air-conditioned rooms, this guesthouse is located on the quiet island of Čiovo near Trogir town.

Villa Sikaa

Obala kralja Zvonimira 10; tel: 021-881 223; www.vila-sikaa-r.com; €€€
Located just outside the Old Town, Villa Sikaa has gradually expanded to accommodate an ever-increasing group of satisfied customers. The staff go out of their way for guests, and the rooms are fitted out with an array of comfort-making amenities, such as internet access, extra-modern shower jets and top-quality mattresses.

Central Dalmatia: Makarska

Hotel Biokovo

Obala K. Tomislava bb; tel: 021-615 244; www.hotelbiokovo.hr; €€
Situated right on the seafront just 150m/yds from the town's pebble beach, this is a decent hotel in a charming location. A recent renovation has seen the addition of a wellness centre and new rooms with internet connection and air-conditioning. Ask for a room with a balcony to enjoy the views.

Central Dalmatia: Vis

Hotel Issa

Šetalište Zanelle 5; tel: 021-711 164; www.vis-hoteli.hr; €€
With 125 rooms, Hotel Issa is larger than its sister hotel, the Tamaris, but is slightly more down-at-heel. It is located on the western part of Vis harbour in a more modern building, and while the rooms are adequate, do not expect too many extras. If they are important to you, check that your room has air-conditioning and/or TV.

Hotel Paula

Petra Hektorovića; tel: 021-711 362; www.hotelpaula.com; €€
The best hotel on Vis is a remarkably stylish affair for such a rustic island. Located on a charming alleyway in the old part of Vis, the attractive, individually decorated rooms all have TV, and some even have kitchenettes. If you are arriving under your own sail, you can moor your boat next to the hotel. The hotel restaurant turns out some delicious local dishes.

Hotel Tamaris

Obala sv. Jurja 30; tel: 021-711 350; www.vis-hoteli.hr; €€
It may be quite basic, but this three-star hotel is small (there are just 25 rooms) and comfortable and housed in an attractive, late 19th-century building overlooking Vis harbour. Bathrooms have showers only. It also has some attic appartments for rent and a lovely waterfront restaurant.

Central Dalmatia: Hvar

Hotel Palace

Trg sv. Sjepana; tel: 021-750 750; www.suncanihvar.hr; €€€
Located just off the main square, this three-star hotel overlooks the bustling harbour. The classical exterior is a real standout and gives a good introduction to the interior; the rooms are beautifully decorated and include air-conditioning, minibar and fine furnishings. The hotel also offers an indoor sea-water pool, sauna and massage, and the staff are efficient and friendly .

Above from far left: Split waterfront; Riva Hvar Yacht Harbor Hotel *(see p.114)*.

Camping
Most campsites are open May–Sept, although a few operate all year. They range from large autocamps with loads of facilities to smaller camps in pretty locations. A good online guide is www.camping.hr.

On the islands, private rooms (most with self-catering facilities and ensuite bathrooms) are a good bet, and hosts are very welcoming and hospitable. There are hundreds of agencies handling accommodation rentals in Croatia. A good place to start is at the National Tourist Board website, www.croatia.hr. Listed under each destination are local tourist offices and travel agencies to contact for referrals. If you arrive without a reservation, head to the local tourist office or look for signs saying *sobe* (rooms). In August, when the coast is inundated with Italians, vacancies can be scarce.

Hotel Pod Stine

Pod Stine bb; tel: 021-740 400; www.podstine.com; €€€

This family-run hotel is a 20-minute walk along the coast from town, but the owners can easily arrange for transport from the bus station or ferry port. The surroundings are spectacular. The terrace restaurant, which offers tasty local specialities at a reasonable price, overlooks a pebble beach, backed by palms, pines and lemon trees. Many rooms have views of the Pakleni Islands, lying just offshore.

Riva Hvar Yacht Harbor Hotel

Obala Oslobidjenja bb; tel: 021-750 750; www.suncanihvar.hr; €€€€

With its great location, the venerable Hotel Riva was always the hotel of choice for the trendsetters who flocked to Hvar Town. However, they really needed something more than just prime real estate and now they have it. The hotel underwent a total metamorphosis to become the Riva Hvar Yacht Harbor Hotel, one of Croatia's finest hotels, displaying the latest in luxury and upmarket style.

Southern Dalmatia: Dubrovnik

Dubrovnik President

Iva Dulčića 39; tel: 020-441 100; www.valamar.com; €€€€

This large four-star hotel is by far the best one on the Babin Kuk peninsula. Classy and beautifully decorated, the Dubrovnik President has what may be Dubrovnik's best beach, a well-maintained stretch of smooth pebbles on a quiet cove. All the rooms have large terraces with sweeping views of the sea. The President also regularly hosts music nights that feature local artists playing in a variety of styles.

Grand Villa Argentina

Put Frana Supila 14; tel: 020-440 555; www.gva.hr; €€€€

With its five-star rating, the Grand Villa Argentina has welcomed journalists, celebrities and politicians for decades. Although not new, the hotel has been continually upgraded and modernised to cater to the tastes of an increasingly elite clientele. The large complex includes four villas and a hotel, all at the highest levels of luxury. There are pools, a spa, private sea access, and it is only a short walk from the Old Town.

Hotel Splendid

Masarykov Put 10; tel: 020-433 560; www.hotelimaestral.hr; €€€

Situated on the Lapad peninsula, at the edge of a small, private cove, this is a good mid-range choice. Rooms are spacious and flawlessly maintained, albeit lacking in decorative flourishes. All rooms are quiet, but try to get a room overlooking the sea. A nearby bus stop means it is easy to get to town and back.

Price for two people sharing a double room in peak season:	
€€€€	over 220 euros
€€€	160–220 euros
€€	90–160 euros
€	below 90 euros

Hotel Sumratin

Šetalište kralja Zvonimira 31; tel: 020-438 930; www.hotels-sumratin.com; €

This modest two-star hotel is a real find in pricey Dubrovnik. Do not expect too many extras (like air-conditioning) in your room, but you will get the necessities. Plus, the hotel has a lovely garden and is well-located on one of the most dynamic streets on the Lapad peninsula, replete with bars, cafés and restaurants.

Hotel Vis

Masarykov Put 4; tel: 020-433 555; www.hotelimaestral.com; €€

Right on the Lapad peninsula, this large hotel is ideal for families. Prices are reasonable, and the hotel beach is nearby and well equipped with water sports facilities to entertain kids of all ages. It is just a 15-minute walk to Dubrovnik Old Town, but there is also a bus stop nearby.

Villa Wolff

Nika i Meda Pucica 1; tel: 021-438 710; www.villa-wolff.hr; €€€

This boutique hotel is in a busy part of Lapad, but manages to create a quiet atmosphere for its guests. Each attractively decorated room has a private terrace with a view of the sea, which is close by, as are many restaurants and cafés.

Southern Dalmatia: Mljet
Hotel Odisej

Pomena; tel: 020-744 022; www.hotelodisej.hr; €€

Mljet's only hotel stands on the northern side of the island in quiet Pomena, just outside the entrance to the national park. The rooms are nothing special, but the low-rise hotel has a wonderful fixed-price buffet lunch, rents bicycles and offers a wealth of information about visiting the park. A 20-minute walk brings you to the lake of Malo Jezero, and you are also close to the harbour restaurants. The hotel also offers two two-bed apartments.

Southern Dalmatia: Korčula
Hotel Marco Polo

Korčula Town; tel: 020-726 131; www.korcula.net; €€€

Large but quite comfortable, this is easily the best hotel accommodation on Korčula. Located on a hill, with lovely views of the town, it well merits its four-star status, with modern furnishings and carpets in the rooms and public areas. The ambience is quiet and business-like. There is also an indoor swimming pool and conference facilities.

Pansion Bebič

Lumbarda; tel: 020-712 505; www.bebic.hr; €

Those tired of cookie-cutter hotels and eager to get behind the scenes to experience a more authentic Korčula should try Pansion Bebić. The multi-lingual Bebić family has welcomed guests for years and add a personal touch to everything, from the well-appointed rooms to the delicious meals served on their delightful terrace-restaurant.

Above from far left: Hvar Town; Grand Villa Argentina, Dubrovnik.

Dubrovnik Neighbourhoods
There are only two hotels in the Old Town, but there are also advantages to staying in other neighbourhoods. East of town in the Ploče neighbourhood, you are only a few minutes' walk from Ploče Gate. Lapad is a leafy peninsula with beaches and is a short drive or bus ride from the Old Town. Babin Kuk is a few minutes further but also provides a calm environment.

Croatians place a strong priority on eating well and expect restaurants to reach a high standard of quality. There is not yet much of a taste for exotic food, so there is a certain sameness to the menus. Fish is almost always grilled in olive oil, garlic and lemon juice, black risotto is on nearly every menu along the coast, and the main vegetable is likely to be *blitva* (swiss chard). Restaurants in Zagreb and, recently, in Dubrovnik tend to be more adventurous – and expensive.

Zagreb: Upper Town

Baltazar

Nova Ves 4; tel: 01-466 6999; www.restoran-baltazar.hr; Mon–Sat lunch and dinner; €€

Baltazar has been an standby for special occasions for many years, but standards remain high. Most of the produce is local, whether it is veal or fresh fish. Vegetarians may not be pleased with the heavy emphasis on meat, but a special vegetable plate can always be arranged. This is also a great place to taste Croatian wines, as the wine cellar is well stocked with Plavac, Grk, Malvasija and other Croatian wines.

Price guide for an average meal for two, with a glass of house wine:

€€€€	over 400Kn
€€€	250–400Kn
€€	150–250Kn
€	below 150Kn

Dubravkin Put

Dubravkin Put 2; tel: 01-483 4970; daily 10am–midnight; €€€€

This is the best fish restaurant in town, as numerous culinary awards have testified. The setting is exquisite, on the edge of Tušanac Park. In fine weather it is a pleasure to enjoy your meal on a leafy terrace. In cooler weather, you can appreciate the modern art decorating the elegant dining room. Wherever you sit, prepare to be dazzled by the amazing cuisine.

Kaptolska Klet

Kaptol 5; tel: 01-481 4838; www.kaptolska-klet.com; daily 10am–midnight; €€

Situated opposite the cathedral, Kaptolska Klet is a vast, welcoming space that offers a robust Zagorje menu including something for everyone. Most dishes are hearty meat dishes guaranteed to warm you on cold winter nights, but there are also lighter vegetarian dishes such as grilled vegetables and a vegetarian loaf. During the summer there is a delightful beer garden to eat in.

Pod Gričkim Topom

Zakmardijeve Stube 5; tel: 01-483 3607; Mon–Sat noon–midnight; €€

Up in Gornji grad, near the funicular station, this informal restaurant has the best location in the city, with fantastic views over the Lower Town. The good Croatian food equals the surroundings with an emphasis on hearty portions of fish. There are also Dalmatian specialities, plus risotto and pasta dishes.

Fellini

Savska 90; tel. 01-617 7545;
www.fellini.hr; daily 11am–midnight; €

All-Italian all the time is the theme here, and it makes a welcome change from the predominating Zagreb and Zagorje cuisine. From healthy antipasti to the kind of pasta dishes they turn out in Trastevere, all is good, authentic and reasonably priced in this casual restaurant.

Medvedgrad Pivnica

Savska Cesta 56; tel: 01-617 7110;
www.pivnica-medvedgrad.hr; daily
10am–midnight; €–€€

This is the most popular and biggest pub in town. Home-made sausages, roast meats, grills, schnitzels and a range of good salads are complemented by a choice of five beers that are brewed on the premises. The atmosphere is relaxed and convivial, and the crowd includes everyone from young professionals to students.

Paviljon

Trg Kralja Tomislava 22; tel: 01-481 3066; www.restaurant-paviljon.com; Mon–Sat lunch and dinner; €€€

An elegant restaurant that is located in a picturesque park and is perfect for celebrating a special occasion. Local chef Stanko Erceg creates exquisite dishes that draw on Croatia's finest ingredients. His signature dish is crispy roast duck on a bed of red cabbage and figs. The restaurant is a favoured haunt of Croatia's celebrities, politicians and diplomats.

Stari Fijaker 900

Mesnička 6; tel: 01-483 3829; Mon–Sat 7am–11pm, Sun 10am–10pm; €€

This traditional spot has long been a meeting place for artists, revolutionaries and family dinners, mainly because of the hearty Zagorje specialities prepared the way granny did. Turkey with *mlinci* (baked noodles), *štrukli* (cheese dumplings), *punjene paprike* (stuffed peppers), bean soups – the menu includes all the staples of northern Croatian cuisine.

Istra

Milanovića 30; tel: 052-434 636;
Mon–Sat 10am–midnight; €€

Whether in the intimate dining rooms or on the terrace, you will feast well at this rustic establishment, popular with the locals. Try the lobster with noodles, cuttlefish *buzara* (in a tomato sauce) or fish *pod pekom* (cooked under a baking lid). In mild weather, it is pleasant to eat outdoors on the covered terrace.

Konoba Ulixes

Dekumanus 2; tel: 052-451 132;
Mon–Sat noon–midnight; €€€

Looking for something a little different? The Croatian dishes here are always served with a special touch. Taste seasonal products like asparagus or truffles, or try the unusual frogfish cooked in a seafood and prosecco sauce. The wine list focuses on the wonderful wines from Istria, and the waiters are happy to help you select the right one for your meal.

Above from far left: fresh beetroot from Zagreb's Dolac market; seafood is one of the chief delights of dining on the Croatian coast; coffee and cake in Zagreb.

Cover Charges
Do not be surprised to see an additional 7–10Kn on your bill at the end of the meal. It is the 'bread charge' that appears whether or not you ate the bread. Restaurants are supposed to indicate this supplement on the menu, but some do not. If you pay in cash you may be able to get the restaurant to waive the charge.

Pizzeria Nono

Zagrebačka 4; tel: 052-453 088; daily noon–midnight; €

Whether it is because of the crowds of Italians flocking to the coast, the Italians that once ruled the coast or the fact that so many Croatians have worked in Italy, Croatian pizza can hold its own next to Italy's best. Even though there are savoury pasta dishes and hearty salads, this is everyone's favourite pizza place. The puffy, thick-crusted bases are always topped with the finest ingredients.

Sv. Nikola

Obala maršala Tita 23; tel: 052-423 018; www.svnikola.com; daily 9am–midnight; €€

The dining is fine indeed in this elegant restaurant. There are two set menus: a fish menu that includes lobster, and a meat menu that includes steak, but both are likely to include carpaccio and truffles in some form. Highly popular with Italians, as truffles are much more expensive in Italy.

Istria: Rovinj

Giannino

A Ferri 38; tel: 052-813 402; daily 11am–midnight; €€

Price guide for an average meal for two, with a glass of house wine:

€€€€ over 400Kn
€€€ 250–400Kn
€€ 150–250Kn
€ below 150Kn

Many are the seafood restaurants along the harbour of Rovinj. With menus in four languages and touts urging you indoors, the price-quality ratio is not the best. Move on. Giannino serves first-rate fish and seafood in a secluded street away from the main tourist area. The sole with truffles is outstanding, but everything on the menu is cooked to perfection.

Istria: Pula

Kantina

Flantička 16; tel: 052-214 054; Mon–Sat 7am–midnight; €€

Dining in the town centre of Pula offers few options, as most residents prefer to head out to the Verudela peninsula. Kantina is the best option in town. Steak with truffles, stuffed turkey breast and ravioli stuffed with cheese and ham are popular dishes. It is an appropriately Austrian menu for a restaurant that occupies a restored Austro-Hungarian building.

Milan

Stoja 4; tel: 052-300 200; daily 11am–midnight; www.milan1967.hr; €€€

Part of a respected hotel, Milan is not far from the town centre. The menu concentrates on fish (choose your from the display on ice, fishmonger-style) and the wine cellar is superb. It is an excellent place to try the best Istrian wines.

Valsabbion

Pješčana Uvala IX/26; tel: 052-218 033; www.valsabbion.hr; daily noon–midnight; €€€€

This is an outstanding, award-winning restaurant and one of the country's best. Everyone from Croatia's Prime Minister to hearthrob Goran Visnjic has eaten here, enjoying the Dalmatian staples and succulent Mediterranean-inspired dishes that are without doubt some of the most imaginative concoctions in the region. Finish off with the outstanding black-and-white mousse.

Vela Nera
Pješčana uvala bb; tel: 052-219 209; daily 8am–midnight; €€€
If a local invites you to a special meal, it may well be here at Vela Nera, where the dining is more casual but still gives Valsabbion a run for its money. On a terrace overlooking the sea, you can savour grouper and aubergine salad, prawns with truffles and other delicious fish and seafood dishes.

Istria: Vodnjan

Gostiona-Trattoria Vodnjanka
Istarska bb; tel: 052-511 435; Mon–Sat 10am–1am; €€
Istrians are justifiably proud of their excellent produce. The rustic setting in this spacious manor perfectly suits the rustic food with ingredients fresh from the Istrian countryside. Naturally there are truffles, but do not miss the wonderful asparagus when it is in season, usually in early spring.

Istria: Roč

Ročka Konoba
Roč; tel: 052-66 645; Tue–Sat lunch and dinner; €€

Very homespun and serving up home-made Istrian sausages and other Istrian dishes, such as *gulaš sa jnokima* (goulash with gnocchi), this is the place Istrians come to when they want to get away from the coastal madness. In summer, sip some of their homemade wine on the terrace.

Central Dalmatia: Split

Bekan
Ivana Zajca 1; tel: 021-389 400; daily noon–midnight; €€
Bekan's terrace overlooks the sea, and the relaxed atmosphere is complemented by wonderful Dalmatian fish and seafood specialities (try the shrimp *buzara*). To get here, head south out of town past the port and Bačvice Beach until Put Firule becomes Ivana Zajca.

Kod Joze
Sredmanuška 4; tel: 021-347 397; daily; €–€€
A typical *konoba* just outside the palace walls, with good risotto, pasta and fish served either in a warm rustic interior or on a terrace in summer. Locals love this place, perhaps because it's somewhat hidden from the tourist circuit. The green tagliatelle with seafood in a creamy sauce is a delight.

Central Dalmatia: Trogir

Čelica
Obala kralja Zvonimira; tel: 021-882 344; daily lunch and dinner; €€
This is Trogir's most romantic choice as the restaurant is on a boat in the Trogir channel. The menu leans to fish and seafood, of course.

Above from far left: beachfront restaurant at Markarska; peaches at a market in Rovinj; a glass of Croatian white; restaurants and cafés line the Riva in Split.

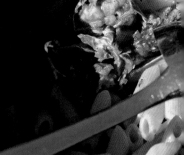

Konoba Menego

Tel: 021-742 036; www.menego.hr;
daily noon–midnight; €€

Despite the influx of tourists, Konoba Menego remains a local favourite committed to using all the wonderful products from Hvar Island. The preparation is traditional, with few fancy touches. Expect smoked meat and cheese, hearty stuffed breads and a liberal use of local olive oil. The restaurant is well signposted from the left side of Hvar's main square.

Macondo

Groda bb; tel: 021-742 850; daily
noon–midnight; €€€

Hvar's best-known fish restaurant is hidden in a narrow alley between the main square and the fortress; just follow the signs from Trg sv. Stjepana to find it. The waiter will tell you what has been caught that day and what is on the menu. Expect dishes such as fish pâté, octopus salad, seafood risotto, lobster spaghetti and fish fillet with roasted vegetables.

Konoba Bako

Gundulićeva 1, Komiža; tel: 021-
713 008; www.konobabako.hr;
daily 11am–midnight; €€

The tiny fishing village of Komiža can easily put you in the mood for fish and seafood, and this family-run establishment serves up the very finest. It is a casual place overlooking a tiny bay with tables at the water's edge. The stone interior contains a fish pond and an archaeological collection that includes Greek and Roman amphorae.

Atlas Club Nautica

Brsalje 3; tel: 020-442 526; daily
11am–11pm; €€€€

A smart restaurant in a fine location, with two terraces overlooking the Lawrence Fort and Bokar Tower, plus tables out in the square. It does less expensive 'light lunches' as well as very pricey dinners, when men are expected to wear a jacket and tie. From November to April you will get 20 per cent off your bill if you pay it in cash.

Gil's

Sv. Dominika bb; tel: 020-322 222;
www.gilsdubrovnik.com; Mar–Dec
noon–11pm; €€€€

Dubrovnik's dining scene has certainly been stirred up by this flashy restaurant. The chef is French, the style is French Fusion and the ingredients run to beluga caviar, oysters and exotic spices. However, Russian oil magnates, business people on expense accounts and owners of mega-yachts are not the only clientele. In the

Price guide for an average meal for two, with a glass of house wine:

€€€€	over 400Kn
€€€	250–400Kn
€€	150–250Kn
€	below 150Kn

informal and ultra-hip Pop Lounge, tapas from around the world are served at a very reasonable price, while DJs spin ambient grooves.

Jadran

Poljana P. Miličevića 1; tel: 020-323 405; daily 9am–1am; €–€€

This large eatery fills the south and east sides of the former Convent of the Poor Clares. Though you eat under austere arches and columns, there is nothing monastic about the enormous menu. Food is straightforward – meat and fish grills, mussels, spaghetti – and there is lots of room to spread out your shopping bags.

Kamenica

Gundulićeva poljana 8; tel: 020-421 499; daily 10am–11pm; €€

Friendly Kamenica has nearly taken over pretty Gundulić Square with its endless rows of tables. Given its wonderful setting and reasonable prices, it is small wonder that it has become so popular. The speciality is mussels, but there are good deals on other ultra-simple seafood dishes.

Mea Culpa

Za Rokom 3; tel: 020-424 819; daily noon to midnight; €

After a hard day at the beach, build up strength with one of Mea Culpa's huge and delicious pizzas. The ingredients are incredibly fresh and tasty whether your pizza is topped with ham, seafood or vegetables. The interior is cosy and there are tables outside. The restaurant is located in a narrow street off Stradun.

Orsan

Od Tabakarije 1; tel: 020-414 188; Easter–mid-Oct noon–midnight; €€

This is a lovely quiet spot in Kolorina cove just a few yards from Pile Gate (*orsan* means boathouse). The fish platters are veritable cornucopias, and the risotto is renowned. Service can be slightly slow, but the sound of waves lapping the walls a few steps away puts you in a very relaxed mood.

Proto

Široka ulica 1; tel: 020-323 324; www.esculap-teo.hr/restaurant_ proto.html; daily 11am–11pm; €€€

A well-established, elegant spot just off Stradun, where Edward VIII and Wallis Simpson dined on their night in Dubrovnik in 1936. You can eat on the street or on the upstairs terrace and the fish dishes are the best you will find. Try the *brodetto* (fish stew) with polenta or the Adriatic shrimp with parsley sauce. Meat and vegetarian dishes are also available.

Rozarij

Marija Sjekavika 4 (corner of Prijeko); tel: 020-423 791; daily noon– midnight; €€

Undoubtedly the best of the Prijeko restaurants, this is most certainly *the* spot for a romantic candlelit dinner. Rozarij serves up excellent Dalmatian food in a cosy dining room or at a few little tables in a leafy corner outside. Try the seafood stew, which includes shrimp, mussels and fish in a savoury and fragrant broth.

Above from far left: brewed in Zagreb; mouth-watering lobster pasta; alfresco drinks in Hvar Town.

The Croatian coast is a fine place to sit and watch the sun rise over the sea after partying all night. Outdoor nightlife starts in April and reaches a peak in July and August with myriad festivals as well as all-night beach parties. The most fun is to be had on the islands, especially Hvar, where locals seem to have a higher level of noise tolerance, plus the capacity to stay out all night and still function in the morning. For the rest of the year, Zagreb and Split have the most varied nightlife offerings.

In the summer many resorts offer open-air cinema; films are usually shown in their original versions, with Croatian subtitles. The local tourist offices have the schedules.

The clubs, bars and concert venues listed are all accessible from places in the itineraries. As Croatia shakes off the ennui of Yugoslavia and the angst of war, more and more venues are opening.

Zagreb

The main centre for bars is in Tkalčićeva in the Upper Town and Bogovićeva in the Lower Town. For entertainment listings, see the monthly *Events and Performances* or the bimonthly *In Your Pocket: Zagreb*, both available free in hotels and tourist offices. For more listings, see p.29.

Aquarius

Matije Ljubeka bb; www.aquarius.hr

Zagreb's biggest nightclub lies 4km (3 miles) from the centre, overlooking Lake Jarun. It has been a Zagreb institution for many years and is an obligatory stop for nightcrawlers of all ages. Dance, commercial and techno predominate on the dance floor, but there are also special-events nights involving fashion and product launches. Dress smart.

Saloon

Tuškanac 1a; www.saloon.hr

Croatian stars hang out at this glamorous, centrally located nightclub, which regularly features in the newspapers' gossip columns. The music is handled by the city's hottest DJs, and there is something going on nearly every night of the week.

Tvornica

Šubićeva 2; www.tvornica-kulture.hr

Host to Wu-Tang Clan, Jane Birkin, Buena Vista Social Club, David Byrne and John Cale among others, this exciting venue presents an adventurous programme of concerts, performance art, plays, exhibitions and dazzling shows. If there was ever any doubt that Zagreb has a cutting-edge nightlife scene, this club has dispelled it.

Vastroslav Lisinski Concert Hall

Trg Stjepana Radića 4; tel: 01-612 1166; www.lisinski.hr

As befits any major European capital, Zagreb has a first-class concert hall to accommodate its culture-loving citizens. There's not much going on in summer as most of the town heads down to the coast, but starting in September there is a full schedule of opera, concerts and ballet.

Istria: Pula

Rock Club Uljanik
Dobrilina 2

In a building overlooking the shipyard, this immensely popular club presents live concerts by Croatia's best rockers. Although mainly frequented by students, all ages will feel welcome. Plus, Uljanik is one of the few venues accessible by foot from central Pula.

Istria: Rovinj

Monvi
Luje Adamovića bb; www.monvi center.com; June–Sept

Strolling through Rovinj you would think that everyone goes straight to bed after sunset. Not so. They head a few kilometres out of town to this vast nightclub complex with open-air concerts, international DJs, a cocktail bar and various restaurants.

Zanzi Bar
Obala Pino Budicin

Watching the sunset from Rovinj could be the highlight of your trip to Croatia, and Zanzi Bar is the place to do it. Chill-out music sets a mellow mood as a well-dressed clientele sips fruity cocktails in this beautifully arranged cocktail bar with open-air seating. If you feel like chomping a cigar, you can buy the best here.

Central Dalmatia: Split

Discovery
Bačvica Bay

Ground zero for Split nightlife is the Bačvice complex, 1km (⅔ mile) south of the Old Town. This network of clubs, bars and cafés overlooks Bačvice Beach, Split's public beach. Discovery is a pulsating disco under the complex, where a cross-section of Split society dance until the small hours.

Ghetto Club
Dosud 10

The young waiters drift pleasantly through the candlelit courtyard, where the music is soft and accompanied by a trickling fountain. From early morning to well past midnight, Ghetto Club provides a relaxing ambience in which to sip drinks and nibble on snacks.

Central Dalmatia: Hvar

Carpe Diem
Riva bb; www.carpe-diem-hvar.com

This cocktail bar has achieved near-legendary status. Almost every celebrity whose yacht docks offshore heads right to Carpe Diem, where, somehow, there always seems to be a camera waiting. From the open-air terrace, it is easy to take in the parade of young socialites in designer beachwear and sunglasses. The cocktails are pricey, but the DJs are Croatia's finest.

Southern Dalmatia: Dubrovnik

Latino Club Fuego
Starcevica 2

Conveniently located just outside Pile Gate, this place never seems to go out of style. Despite the name, the dance music is eclectic, so you can bust your moves to a range of sounds from chart music to vintage disco and the latest house. Dress is casual.

CREDITS

Insight Step by Step Croatia
Written by: Jeanne Oliver and Jane Foster
Edited by: Alex Knights
Series Editor: Clare Peel
Cartography Editors: Zoë Goodwin and James Macdonald
Picture Manager: Steven Lawrence
Art Editor: Ian Spick
Production: Kenneth Chan
Principal photographer: Corrie Wingate
Photography: All by Corrie Wingate/APA, Gregory Wrona/APA and Glyn Genin/APA, except: akg images 22, 37; Ingolf Pompe 41/alamy 18; Bridgeman Art Library 83TR; Jon Jones/Corbis 23; iStockphoto 10–11, 66TL, 122; Leonardo 108, 113, 114, 115.
Front cover: main image: 4corners; bottom left: iStockphoto; bottom right: Gregory Wrona/APA.

Printed by: Insight Print Services (Pte) Ltd, 38 Joo Koon Road, Singapore 628990

First Edition 2009

DISTRIBUTION

Worldwide
Apa Publications GmbH & Co. Verlag KG (Singapore branch), 38 Joo Koon Road, Singapore 628990
Tel: (65) 6865 1600
Fax: (65) 6861 6438

UK and Ireland
GeoCenter International Ltd
Meridian House, Churchill Way West, Basingstoke, Hampshire, RG21 6YR
Tel: (44) 01256 817 987
Fax: (44) 01256 817 988

United States
Langenscheidt Publishers, Inc.
36–36 33rd Street, 4th Floor, Long Island City, NY 11106
Tel: (1) 718 784 0055
Fax: (1) 718 784 0640

Australia
Universal Publishers
1 Waterloo Road, Macquarie Park, NSW 2113
Tel: (61) 2 9857 3700
Fax: (61) 2 9888 9074

New Zealand
Hema Maps New Zealand Ltd (HNZ)
Unit 2, 10 Cryers Road, East Tamaki, Auckland 2013
Tel: (64) 9 273 6459
Fax: (64) 9 273 6479

CONTACTING THE EDITORS

We would appreciate it if readers would alert us to errors or outdated information by writing to us at insight@apaguide.co.uk or Apa Publications, PO Box 7910, London SE1 1WE, UK.

www.insightguides.com

INDEX

Zagreb

0   400 m
0   400 yds